ESSENTIAL NAPLES AND THE AMALFI COAST

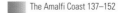

Original text by Jack Altman
Updated by Sally Roy

First published 2007
Revised 2009

ISBN: 978-0-7495-6129-1

Published by AA Publishing, a trading name of AA Media Limited, whose registered office is Fanum House, Basing View, Basingstoke, Hampshire RG21 4EA. Registered number 06112600.

A CIP catalogue record for this book is available from the British Library

Colour separation: MRM Graphics Ltd
Printed and bound in Italy by Printer Trento S.r.l.

A03804

About this book

Symbols are used to denote the following categories:

- map reference to maps on cover
- address or location
- telephone number
- opening times
- admission charge
- restaurant or café on premises or nearby
- nearest underground train station
- nearest bus/tram route
- nearest overground train station
- nearest ferry stop
- nearest airport
- other practical information
- tourist information office
- ➤ indicates the page where you will find a fuller description

This book is divided into five sections.

The essence of Naples and the Amalfi Coast pages 6–19
Introduction; Features; Food and drink; Short break including the 10 Essentials

Planning pages 20–33
Before You Go; Getting There; Getting Around; Being There

Best places to see pages 34–55
The unmissable highlights of any visit to Naples and the Amalfi Coast

Best things to do pages 56–79
Good cafés and restaurants; top activities; stunning views; places to take the children and more

Exploring pages 80–152
The best places to visit in Naples and the Amalfi Coast, organized by area

Maps

All map references are to the maps on the covers. For example, Pompei has the reference *29q* – indicating the grid square in which it is to be found

Admission prices

Inexpensive (under €3)
Moderate (€3–€5)
Expensive (over €5)

Hotel prices

Price are per room per night:
€ budget (under €120);
€€ moderate (€120–€180);
€€€ expensive to luxury (over €180)

Restaurant prices

Price for a three-course meal per person without drinks:
€ budget (under €20);
€€ moderate (€20–€45);
€€€ expensive (over €45)

Contents

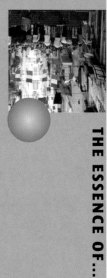

The essence of...

Naples is southern Italy's great city, pulsing with life, full of wonderful buildings and museums and flanked by an idyllic bay. The city is famed as much for its citizens as for its monuments, and there is nowhere else in Italy where you can find such a level of life lived on the streets. The bustle of city life is complemented by the stunning natural beauty of the Amalfi coast with its heady mix of cobalt blue sea, plunging cliffs, and citrus fruit groves. The awesome strength of nature is also evident in the brooding presence of Vesuvius, which destroyed the cities of Ercolano and Pompei.

features

Of all Italian cities, Naples stands supreme in the brilliant way it combines the quintessential image of warm-hearted exuberance with an intriguing darker side. Most of Naples' great art is baroque and that goes for the people, too. Baroque art is imbued with a sense of the melodramatic, of movement and a certain tension. This is as true of outraged butchers and triumphant fishmongers along the Via dei Tribunali as it is of exultant angels and tormented saints in the church of San Gregorio Armeno. People stage a street-corner *sceneggiata* (performance) several times a day for some choice insult, parking ticket or other catastrophe.

Comparing Neapolitans to their monuments is easier now that the *centro storico* (historic centre) is getting a much-needed facelift. But rest assured, for every lovingly restored church or *palazzo*, another is still tottering on in a perversely beautiful state of decay. This juxtaposition of prosperity and poverty gives the city its edge, while its traditions, streetlife and cuisine set it apart from others.

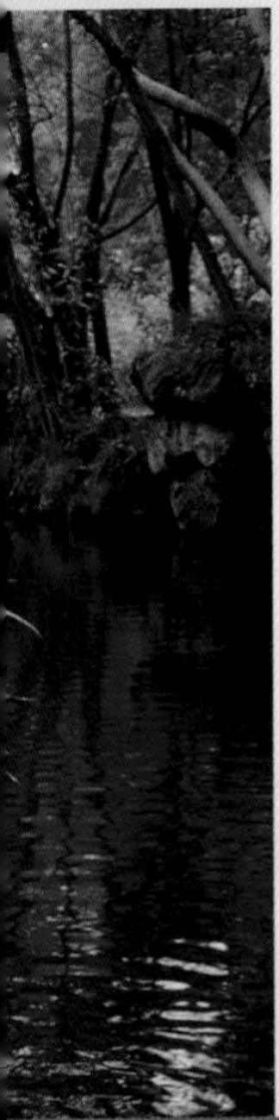

Vesuvius offers the Bay of Naples an enchanting backdrop and an ever-present menace. Pompei, its ancient victim, retains its houses, shops, bakery and brothel. Out in the bay, Capri valiantly protects the charms of its greenery and blue grottoes; while along the Amalfi Coast, a gracious world apart beckons with Ravello's elegant villas, the medieval monuments of Amalfi town, and clusters of houses clinging to the hillside of Positano.

food & drink

Like the best of Italian food, Neapolitan cuisine is simple, savoury and colourful. The tomato is king, the basis of all dishes *alla napolitana*. Historians question whether Naples invented the pizza but nowhere else is it such a gourmet delicacy. And from the Sorrento peninsula and Amalfi Coast comes the great variety of fresh seafood and exquisite mozzarella.

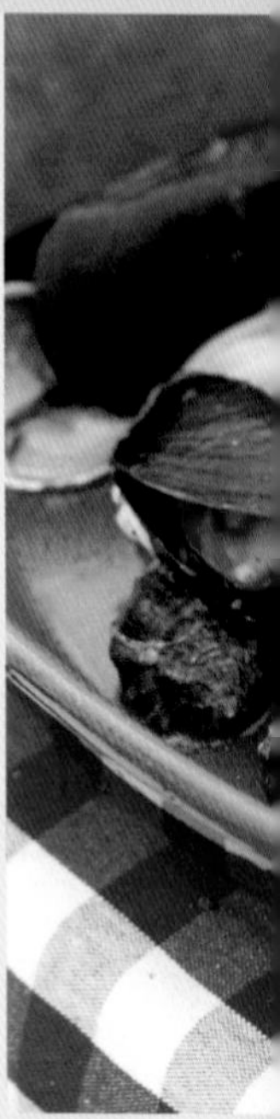

Portions are generous, but in these more health-conscious times, there is no longer the pressure to eat the whole gamut of *antipasti* (starters), a *primo piatto* (first course) of, say, pasta, then a fish or meat *secondo piatto* (second course), followed by fruit, pastry, coffee and a liqueur. Instead you can have a light starter, pasta and salad, and then an ice-cream at a nearby *gelateria*.

STARTERS

Many restaurants offer *bruschetta* (toasted Italian bread) with chopped tomatoes, onions and olives. For more substantial *antipasti*, try a seafood salad of *calamari* (squid), *polpi* (octopus) or *alici* (fresh anchovies); the popular *insalata caprese*, Capri's salad of sliced mozzarella, tomatoes and basil; or a *peperonata* of green, red and

yellow peppers baked in olive oil, onions, tomato and garlic. *Minestra maritata* is a hearty soup of pork or chicken with chicory.

PIZZA AND PASTA

The purists' classical Neapolitan pizza is the *margherita*. First created in 1889 at Naples' Brandi pizzeria (► 108) for Queen Margherita of Savoy, it bears the colours of the Italian flag: red tomatoes, white mozzarella and green basil. Variations are numerous, with seafood, such as *cozze* (mussels), mushrooms, *salsicce* (sausage), scattered with a layer of cold *rucola* (rocket) or the folded *calzone* (pocket pizza), but always with a characteristically thin crust baked in a wood-fired brick oven.

Naples' favourite pasta dishes use simple sauces

of tomato, garlic and olive oil for *vermicelli alla napolitana*, sometimes spiced up with hot red chilli pepper *(all'arrabbiata)*, or melted ricotta cheese for the little spiral *fusilli*. Best known of the seafood sauces is *alle vongole*, with Venus clams. More spectacular is the black pasta *(linguine al nero)* in a delicious sauce of finely chopped squid cooked in its own ink.

FISH AND MEAT DISHES

Best of the locally caught fish are *spigola* (sea bass), *spada* (swordfish), *triglie* (red mullet) or *cefalo* (grey mullet), again served grilled or with a tomato and oregano sauce. Two traditional

Neapolitan beef dishes are *bistecca alla pizzaiola* (sliced beef in a tomato, garlic and oregano sauce), and *braciolone napoletano* (a hearty and filling meat loaf).

DESSERTS

Neapolitan pastries can be a delight: try honeyed *struffoli*, iced chocolate *mustaccioli*, *zeppola* (doughnuts) and sweet ricotta-filled *sfogliatelle*, best with a cappuccino at breakfast.

WINES AND LIQUEURS

The volcanic soil of the Vesuvius vineyards produces some honourable whites, rosés and reds, bottled under the Vesuvio label, as well as the famous *Lacrime di Cristo* dessert wines, fruity and sparkling. White wines from Ravello, Ischia and Capri all go well with seafood. The most popular liqueur, served ice-cold, is the lemon-flavoured *limoncello*, with Sorrento, Amalfi and Capri all claiming to produce the best. Other locally produced liqueurs are *Mirtillo* (bilberry) and *Finocchietto* (fennel).

short break

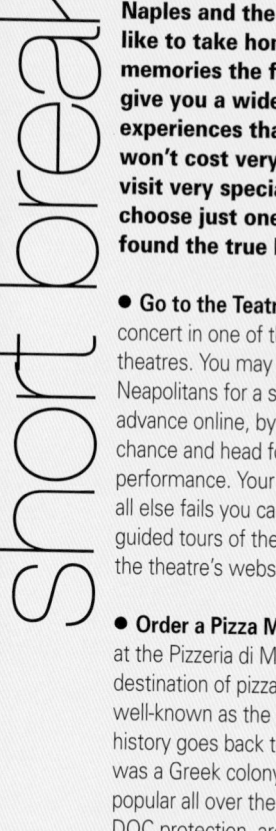

If you have only a short time to visit Naples and the Amalfi Coast and would like to take home some unforgettable memories the following suggestions will give you a wide range of sights and experiences that won't take very long, won't cost very much and will make your visit very special. If you only have time to choose just one of these, you will have found the true heart of the region.

- **Go to the Teatro San Carlo** for an opera or concert in one of the world's most beautiful theatres. You may have to compete with the Neapolitans for a seat, but you can buy tickets in advance online, by fax or phone, or take your chance and head for the box office on the day of a performance. Your hotel may be able to help, but if all else fails you can at least take one of the daily guided tours of the interior (► 105). Also check out the theatre's website – www.teatrosancarlo.it

- **Order a Pizza Margherita,** the classical choice, at the Pizzeria di Matteo on Via dei Tribunali, the destination of pizza gourmets (► 110). Naples is well-known as the home of the pizza, whose history goes back to Greek times when Neapolis was a Greek colony. Although pizzas are now popular all over the world, the best, with their own DOC protection, are still found in Naples.

- **Visit the sumptuous Chapel of San Gennaro** in Naples cathedral, where believers see the blood of the martyred saint liquefy every May and September (► 92). The liquefaction of San Gennaro's blood happened originally just once a year, on the anniversary of its first occurrence one miraculous September day in around AD400.

Suddenly – cynics say in response to popular demand – it also began happening on the saint's feast day in May.

- **Sit at the elegant Caffè Gambrinus** (➤ 60), one of the most famous cafés in Naples, with a cappuccino and crispy *sfogliatella* pastry and watch the world go by on Piazza Trieste e Trento.

- **Escape the turmoil of city traffic** in the gracious convent garden tucked away behind the

Church of San Gregorio Armeno (➤ 90–91). Naples has few tranquil public squares because the Church appropriated all the best open spaces. Here you can sit on a stone bench in the shade of the garden's wonderful citrus trees. In the centre is a marble fountain decorated with dolphins, sea-horses and spouting masks, and flanked by statues of Jesus and the Woman of Samaria.

- **Admire Caravaggio's masterpieces** at the Capodimonte Museum (➤ 44–45) and his altar painting in the Pio Monte della Misericordia church (➤ 98). The couple of years that this violent, brilliant, tormented painter spent in Naples at the end of his life left an indelible mark on the city's art.

- **Take a siesta** under the cooling umbrella pines in the gardens of Ravello's Villa Cimbrone (➤ 145)

or Villa Rufolo (➤ 54–55) and then wake up to the stupendous views of the Amalfi Coast.

- **Stand in the Pompei bakery** and look over the ancient ovens at Vesuvius, brooding on the horizon, quiet for the time being (➤ 40–41). If you are drawn by what you see you can visit the volcano's crater, which is a 30-minute walk from the end of the road.

- **Cruise around Capri** in a boat from Marina Grande harbour and explore the island's many grottoes, not just its most celebrated Grotta Azzurra (➤ 38–39). Also from the harbour, a funicular takes you up to Capri town.

- **Stroll along the cliffs above Positano** (➤ 46–47), from where there are amazing views of Positano and the emerald green sea. When things get too hot it will be hard to resist a swim at one of the beaches below the cliff path.

Planning

Before you go

WHEN TO GO

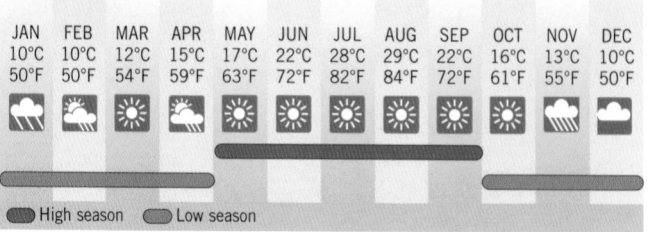

JAN	FEB	MAR	APR	MAY	JUN	JUL	AUG	SEP	OCT	NOV	DEC
10°C	10°C	12°C	15°C	17°C	22°C	28°C	29°C	22°C	16°C	13°C	10°C
50°F	50°F	54°F	59°F	63°F	72°F	82°F	84°F	72°F	61°F	55°F	50°F

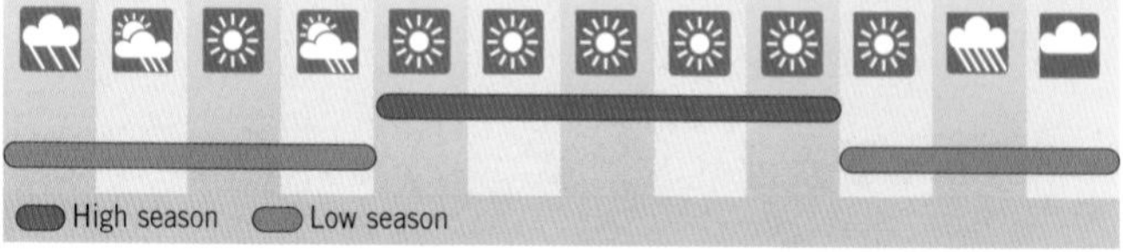

Temperatures are the average daily maximum for each month.

The best time to visit Naples is from May to September, when the temperature range is pleasant and most areas and attractions are not too busy. Within that period, however, expect disruption and increased crowds over the Easter weekend.

August should be avoided, mostly because of the heat but also because many shops, restaurants, clubs and bars close for part of the month.

Although winter can be wet and windy, December is a wonderful month for a visit, with Naples gearing up for Christmas with *presepi* (Christmas cribs) set up in the churches and traditional Christmas gifts and food in the shops.

WHAT YOU NEED

● Required
○ Suggested
▲ Not required

Some countries require a passport to remain valid for a minimum period (usually at least six months) beyond the date of entry – contact their consulate or embassy or your travel agent for details.

	UK	Germany	USA	Netherlands	Spain
Passport (or National Identity Card where applicable)	●	●	●	●	▲
Visa (regulations can change – check before you travel)	▲	▲	▲	▲	▲
Onward or Return Ticket	▲	▲	▲	▲	▲
Health Inoculations (tetanus and polio)	▲	▲	▲	▲	▲
Health Documentation (➤ 23, Health Insurance)	●	●	▲	●	●
Travel Insurance	○	○	○	○	○
Driving Licence (national)	●	●	●	●	●
Car Insurance Certificate (if own car)	○	○	○	○	○
Car Registration Document (if own car)	●	●	●	●	●

WEBSITES

- www.inaples.it (Naples Tourist Board)
- www.enit.it (Italian Tourist Board)
- www.italiantourism.com
- www.comune.napoli.it
- www.napoli.com
- www.amalfitouristoffice.it

TOURIST OFFICES AT HOME

In the UK

Italian State Tourist Board ✉ 1 Princes Street, London W1B 2AY ☎ 020 7408 1254

In the USA

Italian Government Travel Office (ENIT) ✉ 630 Fifth Avenue, Suite 1565, New York NY 10111 ☎ 212/245-5618

Italian Government Travel Office (ENIT) ✉ 12400 Wilshire Boulevard, Suite 550, Los Angeles, CA 90025 ☎ 310/820-1898 or 310/820-9807

HEALTH INSURANCE

Insurance EU nationals receive medical and hospital treatment with the relevant documentation – a European Health Insurance Card (EHIC) for Britons – and pay a percentage for medicines. Medical insurance is still advised. US visitors should check their insurance coverage.

Dental services Nationals of EU countries can obtain dental treatment at reduced cost at dentists which operate within the Italian health service. A qualifying document (EHIC for Britons) is needed. Still, private medical insurance is advised for all. Check out www.ehic.org.uk

TIME DIFFERENCES

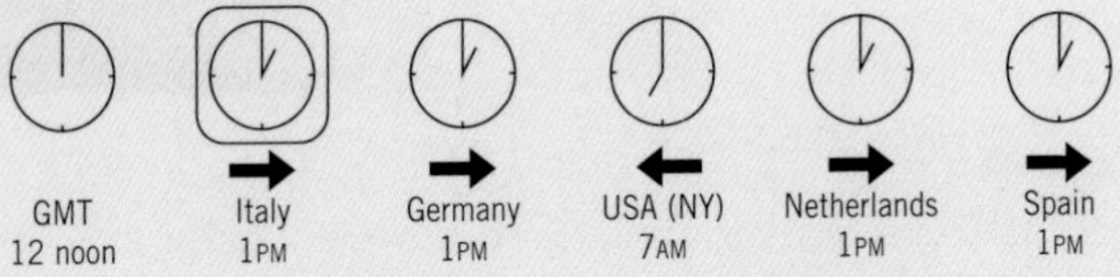

GMT	Italy	Germany	USA (NY)	Netherlands	Spain
12 noon	1PM	1PM	7AM	1PM	1PM

Naples is one hour ahead of GMT, six hours ahead of New York and nine hours ahead of Los Angeles. Clocks go forward one hour for summer time.

NATIONAL HOLIDAYS

1 January *New Year's Day*
6 January *Epiphany*
March/April *Easter Monday*
25 April *Liberation Day*
1 May *Labour Day*
15 August *Assumption (Ferragosto)*
1 November *All Saints' Day*
8 December *Immaculate Conception*
25 December *Christmas Day*
26 December *Santo Stefano*

Most shops and museums close on these days.

WHAT'S ON WHEN

January *Costume Parade* (New Year's Day) in the Piazza Umberto I, Capri.
Procession for Children (Epiphany, 6 Jan). Piazza del Plebiscito, Naples.
Costumed nativity play at Stazione Marittima, Naples.
Burning of Christmas Trees (17 Jan), Naples.
February *Carnival* – five days of parades and parties in Capua.
Carnival – masked parades through *centro storico*, Naples.
April *Easter* – re-enactments of the Stations of the Cross; hooded processions of lay fraternities on Sorrento peninsula.
Pasquetta (Easter Monday) – many Neapolitans take picnicking excursions out to the country.
Pizza baking contest on Naples' Piazza Mercato.
Liberation Day (25 April) – celebration of World War II invasion by the Allies.

May *Labour Day* (1 May).
Maggio Sacro (first Sun) – procession from the Duomo to Santa Chiara, Naples. The first of two annual commemorations of the liquefaction of San Gennaro's blood.
Feast of San Costanzo, in Capri, with processions.
May–August Series of classical music concerts at Villa San Michele, Anacapri.
June *Estate a Napoli* – start of the summer season of classical music in the courtyards of Castel Nuovo, Castel Sant'Elmo and Castel dell'Ovo, Naples.
Jazz concerts in Ravello.
July The summer music festival commemorates Wagner and other composers' residence at the Villa Rufolo, Ravello (➤ 54–55).
Madonna del Carmine is celebrated by fireworks at Piazza Mercato, Naples, simulating the burning of the campanile.
Midnight concerts – start of the summer arts season featuring music, films and cabaret in the public parks.
Sant'Anna (25 Jul) – procession of illuminated boats for the patron saint of Ischia.
August *Ferragosto* (15 Aug) – Assumption Day festivities include music and games throughout Naples. Also procession and fireworks in Positano.
September Pizza festival in Naples.
San Gennaro's Feast Day (19 Sep) – the second commemoration of the liquefaction of the saint's blood in the Duomo, Naples.
October Start of the autumn classical music season at the Conservatory and *palazzo* courtyards, Naples.
November Opera – opening of Teatro San Carlo's opera season, Naples.
Festival Internazionale del Cinema – in Salerno.
December There is a Christmas market on Via San Gregorio Armeno, Naples.
There are general seasonal festivities held throughout the *centro storico* in Naples.

Getting there

BY AIR

Naples (Capodichino) Airport

7km (4.5 miles) from city centre

Train: N/A

Bus: 45 minutes

Taxi: 30 minutes

Alitalia (tel: 06 2222; www.alitalia.it) and British Airways (tel: 0844 493 0787; www.britishairways.com) operate direct flights from London to Naples, as does the budget airline easyJet (www.easyjet.co.uk), and a number of charter airlines, including Thomas Cook (tel: 0844 855 8515; www.thomascookairlines.co.uk), with whom you can make a flight-only reservation. There are no direct scheduled flights to Naples from the USA, Canada, Australia or New Zealand. Travellers from these countries should route through Milan or Rome, then either fly or take the train to Naples.

The Aeroporto Internazionale di Napoli (Capodichino) is linked to the city centre by airport and local buses, and taxis are available outside the terminal. If you are travelling further south, there is a regular bus service as far as Sorrento from the airport (Autolinee Curreri, tel: 081 801 5420; www.curreriviaggi.it). If you arrive in Naples on a package holiday, onward travel to the city should be arranged from the airport by your tour operator.

Alibus (tel: 800 639 525; www.gesac.it) operates between the airport, the Stazione Centrale at Piazza Garibaldi and Piazza Municipio (for the ferry port) 6:30am–11:30 pm daily. Tickets cost €3 and can be purchased on board. The local orange bus 3S runs from the airport every 25 minutes to Piazza Garibaldi; buy tickets (€1) at the news kiosks in the airport and stamp them when you board. Taxis into the city should cost around €13, with an additional charge for luggage.

Travelling south

If you are staying south of Naples take the bus or a taxi to the Stazione Garibaldi, where you can board a Circumvesuviana train (tel: 081 772 2111; www.circumvesuviana.it), a train line serving towns around the Bay of

Naples and terminating in Sorrento. From Sorrento, visitors can connect with buses serving the Sorrento peninsula and the Amalfi coast; these leave from outside Sorrento station and tickets should be purchased from the news kiosk inside the station before boarding. Alternatively, take the airport bus as far as Sorrento, though bear in mind it is a direct service with no stops between the airport and Sorrento.

BY CAR

- Drive on the right.
- Speed limits: motorways (autostrade), for which there are tolls, are 130kph (80mph); main roads 110kph (68mph); secondary roads: 90kph (55mph); urban roads: 50kph (30mph).
- Seat belts must be worn at all times where fitted.
- Random breath-testing is carried out; never drive under the influence of alcohol.
- Outside urban areas petrol stations open 7am to 12:30pm and 3 to 7:30pm. Most close on Sundays. Credit cards are rarely accepted.
- In the event of a breakdown, tel: 116, giving your registration number and type of car and the nearest ACI (Automobile Club d'Italia, www.aci.it) office will assist you. You will be towed to the nearest ACI garage. This service is free to foreign-registered vehicles or cars rented from Rome or Milan airports (you will need your passport).

BY FERRY

Ferry services run from the Molo Beverello to Sorrento, Capri, Ischia and the Amalfi coast. The main operators are Alilauro (tel: 081 497 2238; www.alilauro.it), Caremar (tel: 892 123; www.caremar.it), Metro del Mare (tel: 199 600 700; www.metrodelmare.com) and SNAV (tel: 081 428 5555; www.snav.it). Take the airport bus to Piazza Municipio and walk to the waterfront where you'll find the ticket offices for the various companies, which operate both hydrofoil and ferry services.

BY TRAIN

If you're travelling to Naples by train, most long-distance services arrive at Piazza Garibaldi, which handles the super-fast Alta Velocità, Eurostar and InterCity (Trenitalia – tel: 081 567 2990; www.trenitalia.it). Journey times from Rome to Naples are approximately 2 hours, and 3 hours from Milan.

Getting around

PUBLIC TRANSPORT

Internal flights Services throughout the country are provided by the national airline Alitalia (www.alitalia.it) to Capodichino Airport (tel: 081 789 6259: www.gesac.it). The flight time to Naples from Rome is 60 minutes and from Milan 75–85 minutes.

Trains The national rail network is run by Trenitalia (www.trenitalia.it) sometimes referred to by its former name, the Ferrovie dello Stato. The Intercity train reaches Rome from Naples in 2 hours and the Treno Eurostar is 15 minutes faster. Trains provide good service around the Bay of Naples, the Circumvesuviana to Pompei and Sorrento, and the Cumana to Pozzuoli and Baia.

Regional buses SITA (tel: 081 552 2176; www.sita-on-line.it) provides a good regular service between Naples (Via Pisanelli, near Piazza Municipio) and the Amalfi Coast resorts to Salerno. SEPSA buses (tel: 081 542 9965; www.sepsa.it) leave Piazza Garibaldi for Pozzuoli and Baia.

Boat trips Ferries and the much faster hydrofoils leave from two main piers in Naples' harbours. From Molo Beverello, Caremar (tel: 081 199 123199; www.caremar.it) serves Capri, Ischia and Sorrento. Alilauro (tel: 081 497 2222; www.alilauro.it) serves Ischia from Mergellina. Capri is also linked directly to both Positano and Sorrento.
Urban transport A Unico Napoli ticket is valid for 90 minutes' travel on city buses, trams, metro, funicular, Ferrovia Cumana and Circumflegrea. A day ticket is also available.

TAXIS

Taxis can be hailed, though you'll be lucky to find one passing when you want it. Otherwise find a rank (at stations and *piazze*), or call a radio taxi (in Naples tel: 081 552 5252 or 081 556 4444).

CAR RENTAL

Car rental is not recommended in Naples, due to the city's layout, chaotic driving conditions and lack of parking. If you're heading south, rental is available from international and local companies, but bear in mind that the roads on the Sorrento peninsula and Amalfi coast are vertiginous and twisting, and previous experience of driving in Italy is recommended.

TICKETS AND FARES

Train and internal airline tickets can be bought online, at stations and airports and from some travel agents. In cities, bus and tram tickets must be bought before boarding; tickets are available at *tabacchi* and news agents. Tickets must be validated by stamping them in a special machine before travel commences; these are on station platforms and inside public transport vehicles. There are few travel concessions for foreign visitors.

Visitors to Naples and the Campania region can take advantage of the Campania Artecard, a 3- or 7-day pass, valid for either Naples only or the entire region, giving free entry to all major museums and archaeological sites and reductions to others, plus free access to all public transport in the area, including one ferry trip on the Metro del Mare service. Buy it at the airport, newsagents, railway stations, or any of the museums or archaeological sites.

EU citizens over the age of 65 can get reduced entry rates to museums on production of an identity card (or passport).

Being there

TOURIST OFFICES

✉ Piazza del Gesù Nuovo 7 ☎ 081 552 3328 🕐 Mon–Sat 9–1:30 (Apr–Oct also 3:30–7)

✉ Piazza dei Martiri 58, Chiaia ☎ 081 410 7211 🕐 Mon–Fri 9–2

✉ Via San Carlo 9 ☎ 081 402394 🕐 Apr–Oct Mon–Sat 9–1:30, 3:30–7; Nov–Mar Mon–Sat 9–1:30

Official websites for visitor information: www.inaples.it and www.eptnapoli.info

MONEY

The euro (€) is the legal currency of Italy. Euro notes come in denominations of 5, 10, 20, 50, 100, 200 and 500. Coins are 1, 2, 5 bronze-coloured euro cents and 10, 20 and 50 gold-coloured euro cents. In addition there is a €1 coin with a silver centre and gold surround and a €2 coin with a gold centre and silver surround.

TIPS/GRATUITIES

Yes ✓ No ✕

Restaurants (if service not included)	✓	15–20%
Bars	✓	15–20%
Taxis	✓	15–20%
Porters	✓	€1–€2/bag
Chambermaids	✓	€5–€10/week
Toilets	✕	

POSTAL AND INTERNET SERVICES

Naples's main post office is at Piazza Matteotti (Via Toledo, open Mon–Fri 8–6:30, Sat 8–12:30). Most have long queues and it is better to buy stamps from a *tabaccho*. For sending mail outside Italy, make sure you buy *posta prioritaria* stamps, which will ensure delivery within 3 to 4 days.

Naples and the southern resorts have numerous internet offices, where you'll pay from €5–€10 for every half hour online. All airports and some stations have WiFi areas and some city hotels, 3-star and above, have internet access in bedrooms. In some areas you may find that only dial-up internet access is available and this can be very slow.

TELEPHONES

Telephones are in public places and almost every bar. They take 20 or 50 cent or €1 coins, and more often credit card or phonecards *(schede telefoniche)*, which you can buy for €5 or €10. Phonecards are available from Telecom Italia offices, tobacconists and stations.

Emergency telephone numbers
Police 112
Fire 115
Ambulance 113

International dialling codes
UK 00 44
USA/Canada 00 1
Irish Republic 00 353
Australia 00 61
Germany 00 49
International operator 170

EMBASSIES AND CONSULATES

UK ☎ 081 423 8911
Germany ☎ 081 248 8511
Netherlands ☎ 081 551 3003
Spain ☎ 081 411 157
USA ☎ 081 583 6111

ELECTRICITY

Power supply: 220 volts. Socket: usually round two- hole taking plugs of two round pins. British visitors should bring an adaptor; US visitors will need a voltage transformer.

HEALTH ADVICE

Sun advice From June onwards, the summer sun can get dangerously hot, particularly in unshaded archaeological sites like Pompei. Use plenty of sunscreen, wear a hat and drink lots of water.
Drugs Pharmacies *(farmacia)*, recognized by their green cross sign, have highly trained staff who are able to offer medical advice on minor ailments and provide a wide range of prescription and non-prescription medicines and drugs.

Safe water It is quite safe to drink tap water and water from drinking fountains, but never drink from a tap marked *acqua non potabile*. However, many Italians prefer the taste of bottled mineral water, which is widely available.

PERSONAL SAFETY

The *Carabinieri* (military-style-uniforms and white shoulder belts) deal with general crime and public order. The worst problem (really be on your guard for this) is theft and pickpockets.

- Carry shoulder bags slung across your body.
- Don't wear expensive jewellery or carry large sums of money.
- In the city consider carrying your passport and credit cards in a pouch or belt.
- Keep on the inside of the pavement.
- Lock car doors and never keep valuables in your vehicle.

OPENING HOURS

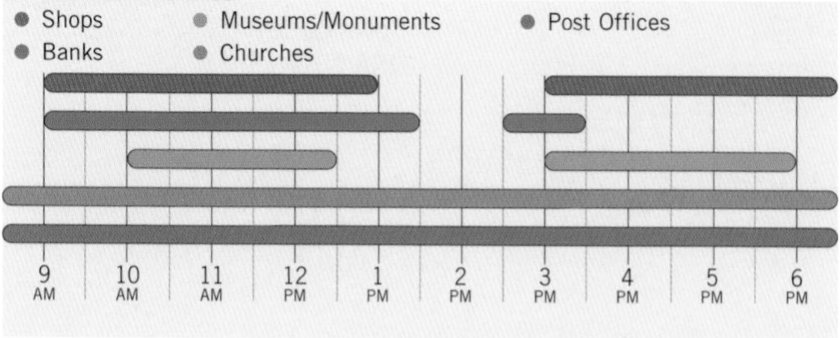

General opening hours for shops are: 9/10–1/1:30 and 3/4–7:30/8. Shops and department stores in tourist areas may stay open all day and later in the evening. Some shops are closed Monday morning, others on Saturday afternoon or all day. Most close on Sunday. Winter opening times may be a little shorter. Banks are closed during lunch (usually 1:20–2:20) and at weekends. Museum times are erratic and should always be checked for changes. Last entries are normally an hour before closing.

LANGUAGE

Italian is the native language, but the Neapolitan dialect may seem like a whole other tongue. Many Italians speak English but you will be better received if you at least attempt to communicate in Italian. Italian words are pronounced phonetically. Every vowel and consonant (except 'h') is sounded. The accent usually (but not always) falls on the penultimate syllable. Below is a list of a few words that may be helpful.

yes	*si*	good afternoon	*buongiorno*
no	*non*	goodnight	*buona sera*
please	*per favore*	how are you ?	*come sta ?*
thank you	*grazie*	do you speak English?	*parla inglese ?*
welcome	*benvenuto*		
hello	*ciao*	I don't understand	*non capisco*
goodbye	*arrivederci*	how much ?	*quanto costa ?*
good morning	*buongiorno*	open/closed	*aperto/chiuso*
bank	*banca*	cheque	*cheque*
exchange office	*cambio*	traveller's cheque	*traveller's cheque*
post office	*ufficio postale*		
coin	*moneta*	credit card	*carta di credito*
banknote	*banconote*	exchange rate	*corse del cambio*
café	*caffè*	beer	*birra*
waiter	*cameriere*	wine	*vino*
waitress	*cameriera*	water	*acqua*
bill	*conto*	coffee	*caffè*
airport	*aeroporto*	boat	*battello*
train	*treno*	ticket	*biglietto*
station	*stazione*	single ticket	*andante*
bus	*autobus*	return ticket	*andante e ritorno*
bus stop	*fermata d'autobus*	car	*machina*
hotel	*albergo*	reservation	*prenotazione*
single room	*singola*	room service	*servizio nella stanza*
double room	*matrimoniale*	toilet	*gabinetto*

Best places to see

1 Duomo di Amalfi

Rising above a monumental stairway, the imposing cathedral is the perfect expression of Amalfi's past as a medieval maritime power.

The oldest part of the largely Romanesque cathedral dates back to the 10th century when Amalfi's ships criss-crossed the Mediterranean to ply their trade with Arab and Persian potentates – and occasionally to plunder the cargoes of rivals from Pisa, Genoa and Venice. The exotic tastes of the eastern Mediterranean are reflected in the Arabian-style interlocking arches and majolica-tiled ornament on the church and its 13th-century campanile set at an angle to the facade. The bronze Byzantine door was made in Constantinople in 1065 by Simeon of Syria and was presented to the city by Pantaleone Di Mauro, an Amalfitan merchant of legendary wealth.

The porticoed atrium at the top of the stairway, rebuilt along with the facade in the 19th century, connects the older Basilica del Crocifisso (Crucifix Basilica) to the main part of the cathedral. Inside the beautifully restored chapel are magnificent examples of gold and silver work, statues and the exquisite marble bas-relief of the Madonna

of the Snow. Completed in 1276, the cathedral was expanded to house the relics of St Andrew in its crypt. The reputed remains of the first Apostle were brought here from Constantinople to be buried under the main altar, designed by Domenico Fontana.

To the left of the atrium, the Chiostro del Paradiso (Cloister of Paradise) was built by Archbishop Filippo Augustariccio in 1266 as a cemetery for the Amalfitan aristocracy. Today, the quadrangle is a haven of quiet, the palm trees and slender-columned, pointed arches another reminder of the city's ancient links with the Middle East.

29r Piazza del Duomo, Amalfi 089 871 059
Apr–Jun daily 9–7; Jul–Sep daily 9–9; Oct–Mar daily 9:30–5:15
Duomo free; Crypt and Chiostro del Paradiso inexpensive
Cafés, restaurants (€–€€€)
Corso Repubbliche Marinare 27
089 871 107

2 Grotta Azzurra, Capri

The iridescent quality of light reflected on water and rock puts this cave, known since Roman times, deservedly among the world's most celebrated natural sights.

A trip to the Blue Grotto may be hackneyed, drawing in visitors by the thousand and being firmly near the top of every tourist's tick-list, but once inside, the intense luminosity of the blue light through the water is truly magical, an effect that instantly explains just what all the fuss is about. This ethereal light is due to the play of sunlight refracted through the narrow opening to the grotto onto the walls and through the sea inside the cave. It's a tiny opening, just 2m (6ft) wide with barely 1m (3ft) of headroom, but inside you'll find yourself in a lofty interior that's 54m (117ft) long and 30m (100ft) wide, with rounded walls rising 15m (50ft) above you.

The Romans knew of this cave, but during the Dark Ages it became associated with evil spirits and locals gave it a wide berth. It was rediscovered in 1826 when a local fisherman ventured in with the German poet Augustus Kopisch and Swiss painter Ernst Fries, who spread the word, and the Blue Grotto became synonymous with Capri.

Take a fast boat from the harbour at Marina Grande along the coast to the entrance, where you'll have to transfer over the side into the specially designed rowing boats that visit the cave; a splendidly Italian experience where the frenzied cries of the boatmen give way to lusty renditions of

O Sole Mio once you're safely inside. A quick tour round and you're ducking your head as the tiny boat leaves. Bear in mind that even slightly agitated sea conditions will make access impossible, so check before you set out and be prepared to wait at anchor at the entrance.

27r Capri Daily 9 to one hour before sunset, but frequently closed due to sea conditions Expensive None From Anacapri Motor boat from Marina Grande, then rowing boat at grotto entrance Not recommended for less agile visitors, or those prone to seasickness

Marina Grande 081 837 0634

3 Monte Vesuvio

www.parconazionaledelvesuvio.it

Serene yet menacing, Vesuvius, overlooking the Bay of Naples, last erupted in 1944 and continues to exert its magnetism on local inhabitants and visitors alike.

The earliest picture of Vesuvius is from a house in ancient Pompei showing a pretty mountain covered in woods and vineyards. That fresco, now in Naples' Museo Archeologico Nazionale (➤ 42–43), was buried in the famous eruption of AD79. Today, 700,000 people live on the slopes, some in houses only a few hundred metres from the crater. More than 2,000 years after it first exploded into life, it looks peaceful enough – no white plume from the

summit and, even up close, just a few steaming fumaroles. But Vesuvius is just sleeping, not dead.

After the Pompei catastrophe, seven major eruptions occurred before 1032 and several minor ones up to the 14th century. The volcano then lay dormant for over 300 years. In 1631, it exploded again, splitting its southern flank and burying 4,000 villagers in molten lava, ash and boiling mud. In recent centuries, the most spectacular eruption came in 1872 when a new cone opened on the north flank. Major 20th-century eruptions occurred in 1906, decapitating the cone and spouting a fountain of gas and lava 600m into the air, and eerily during an Allied bombing raid in 1944.

The volcano today has two peaks, the original Somma (1,132m/3,714ft) and the newer Vesuvio (1,277m/4,190ft), with a crater 600m (1,970ft) wide and 200m (655ft) deep. The road from Ercolano winds through woodland and sombre lava fields to a car park, with a 30-minute walk to the crater. On the way, the **Museo dell'Osservatorio Vesuviano** has audiovisual displays of volcanic activity.

28p Parco Nazionale del Vesuvio Access to crater from sunrise to one hour before sunset Climb to crater moderate Café/restaurant (€) at summit car park
Vesuvio Express from Ercolano (outside station)
Ercolano (Circumvesuviano line from Naples) Guides (moderate) will take you from the carpark to the crater (081 777 5720; www.guidevesuvio.it)
Via IV Novembre 82–84 Ercolano 081 788 1243

Museo dell'Osservatorio Vesuviano
081 610 8483; www.ov.ingv.it Daily 10–2 (by appointment only)

4 Museo Archeologico Nazionale

Proximity to the great Roman sites of southern Italy has enabled Naples to create one of the best endowed archaeological museums in Europe.

Ideally, any projected visit to Pompei and Herculaneum should begin here. In the relative tranquillity of the museum at the top of busy Via Santa Maria Costantinopoli, you can get a sense both of the immense riches of sculpture, painting and mosaics recovered from the buried cities and of comparable treasures brought here from Rome. Like the Capodimonte Museum (► 44–45), the Archaeological Museum was originally founded in 1777 to house the private collections of the Farnese family. To these were added findings from the Roman cities buried by Vesuvius, along with other collections from ancient Greece and Egypt.

The best way to tackle the collection is to start on the first floor, with paintings from Pompei and Herculaneum, and work your way down. First-floor highlights include the famous dual portraits of Paquius Proculus and his wife, a splendid Hercules watching his child Telephus being suckled by a doe, and artwork from Pompei's Temple of Isis. There is also a fine 19th-century detailed scale model of the excavated city of Pompei. On the mezzanine floor are the great mosaics of Alexander the Great defeating Darius of Persia, and exquisite bird and animal scenes. Perhaps most famous of all are the erotic paintings, mosaics and sculpture kept in the adults-only Gabinetto Segreto (Secret Cabinet).

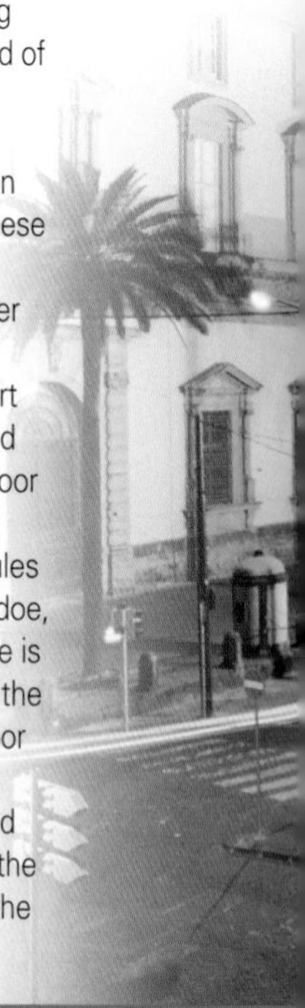

The ground floor's most important pieces are the Roman marble statues from the Farnese collection. *The Tyrannicides*, *Hercules* and *Dirce and the Wild Bull* are invaluable copies of long-lost masterpieces from classical Greece (5th–4th century BC).

7E Piazza Museo Nazionale 19, Napoli 081 442 2149 Mon, Wed–Sun 9–7:30. Last entry 6pm. Closed 1 Jan, 1 May, 25 Dec Expensive, Gabinetto Segreto extra Cafés, restaurants (€–€€) Museo, Piazza Cavour C57, C63, R4 Audio tours and lectures. The Gabinetto Segreto can only be visited by guided tour, advance booking required

5 Museo di Capodimonte

In a hilltop park overlooking the city, the Bourbons' 18th-century palace houses one of Italy's most important art museums.

The Museo di Capodimonte brings art and nature together to provide a soothing escape from the city hustle. After decades of neglect, the collections of predominantly Italian Renaissance and baroque paintings hang once more in the handsomely renovated rooms of the elegant Bourbon palace. The park's landscaped gardens are a bonus: lawns among groves of pine, holm oak, maple and cedar, fragrant eucalyptus and magnolia, and a grand view over the city and Bay of Naples. King Charles of Bourbon (Carlo di Borbone) chose the site in 1739 as hunting grounds and added a porcelain factory (still here). In the palace he hung the art collections of his mother, Elisabetta Farnese, for which the museum was created in 1957.

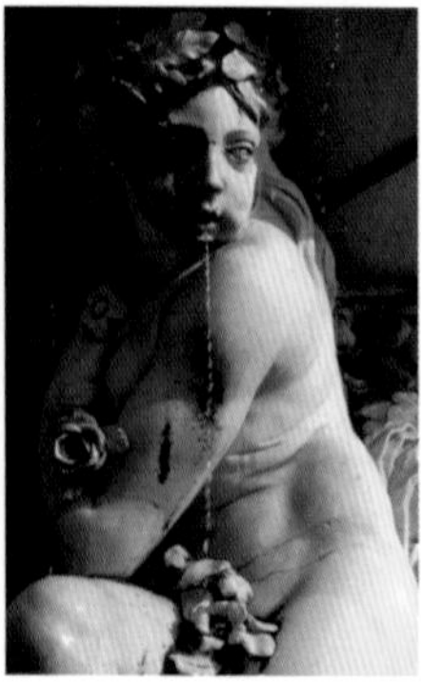

On the first floor, the Farnese Gallery (rooms 2–30) houses several masterpieces of Italian and Flemish art from the 15th–17th centuries. Highlights include Masaccio's *Crucifixion* (1426), Mantegna's portrait of the 16-year-old Cardinal Gonzaga (1461), Titian's sensual *Danae* (1545, hidden from public view in more prudish times), Parmigianino's exquisite *Antea* (1535, now an emblem of Capodimonte), and Pieter Brueghel's

Parable of the Blind (1568). On the same floor (rooms 31–60) are the palace's royal apartments showing fine porcelain and objects of decorative art from the Borgia family collection. The second floor exhibits Neapolitan art with pieces from the city's churches. These include Simone Martini's lovely *St Ludovic of Toulouse* (1317, from San Lorenzo Maggiore, ➤ 100) and Caravaggio's *Flagellation of Christ* (1609, from San Domenico Maggiore). A third floor displays modern art.

7A Via di Miano 2, Napoli 081 749 9111 (recorded information) or 848 800 288 Thu–Tue 8:30–7:30. Park daily 8 to one hour before sunset. Closed 1 Jan, Easter Sun, 1 May, 15 Aug, 25 Dec Expensive; park grounds free Ground-floor café (€) C57, C63, R4

6 Positano

Dazzling white houses tumble down the hillside to the sea at elegant Positano, the coast's most picture perfect resort.

Positano is popularly believed to have been settled by refugees from Paestum (➤ 140–141) – Greek Poseidonia – hence its name. Certainly it shares today with those ancient Greek colonists an undeniable taste for good living. The only monument of note is the originally Romanesque **Church of Santa Maria Assunta,** with a large majolica-tiled dome, added in the 18th century. On the high altar is a 13th-century Byzantine-style Black Madonna, and medieval bas-relief carving on the campanile. Positano is a delightful place in which just to hang out, eat the seafood, shop on Via dei Mulini in the fashionable boutiques and to use as a base for sightseeing.

In high season, to escape the jam-packed alleys and crowded beach at Marina Grande, from where the coastal excursion boats leave, head round the cliff to the rocky beach at Fornillo, guarded on either side by two ancient Saracen watch towers, or head up the precipitous streets to the tiny villages of Montepertuso and Nocella. From here, you can access the

Sentieri degli Dei (Footpath of the Gods), a magnificent trail high above the sea that's not for the faint-hearted. Back down at sea level, you can board local boats that serve the swimming coves of Ciumicello, La Porta and Arienzo.

29r First-class cafés, restaurants (€–€€€) on Marina Grande SITA between Sorrento and Salerno Amalfi Coast (TravelMar 089 872 950)
Via del Saracino 4 089 875 067

Church of Santa Maria Assunta
Via Marina 089 875 480 Daily 8:30–12:30, 3:30–5:30. Closed during services

7 Spaccanapoli, Naples Old Town

The thoroughfare that splits the historic centre of Naples traces the great moments of the city's story – medieval, Renaissance and baroque.

Viewed from the hill of Certosa di San Martino (➤ 89), Spaccanapoli slices through the Naples of mansions, churches and university buildings, each with concealed gardens and cloisters, to the Forcella district of craftsmen's workshops. What was once a main artery of ancient Greek Neapolis today changes its name along the way from Via

Benedetto Croce to Via San Biagio dei Librai, intersected by side streets preserving the grid plan of antiquity. Piazza del Gesù is the entrance to the Graeco–Roman city, where the Jesuits transformed a 15th-century palace into their Church of Gesù Nuovo (► 95). Near by is the fortress-like Church of Santa Chiara and its exquisite cloister-garden (► 100–101).

Palazzo Venezia (No. 19) was the home of the Venetian ambassadors. Via Benedetto Croce opens out onto Piazza San Domenico with its charming café, pastry shop, the Gothic Church of San Domenico Maggiore (► 98–99) and the elegant russet Renaissance facade of the Palazzo Corigliano. Via San Biagio dei Librai is dedicated to the patron saint of booksellers, who had their shops here. The 15th-century Palazzo Carafa Santangeli has a marble portal with Roman statues above its wooden doors. Inside the 16th-century charitable bank of Monte di Pietà is a chapel with a ceiling fresco (1618) by Belisario Corenzio.

8F Via Benedetto Croce, Via San Biagio dei Librai Most churches and several *palazzi* open daily 9–2 Good cafés, restaurants and pizzerias (€–€€) In the pedestrian zone There are informative signposts for principal monuments on the itinerary of the tourist office's *museo aperto* (open museum)

8 Tempio di Nettuno, Paestum

www.infopaestum.it

Best preserved of the ancient monuments in the Greek city of Paestum, this 2,500-year-old temple is a marvel of Doric power and simplicity.

Paestum was originally named Poseidonia and this temple was popularly thought to be dedicated to the city's protective deity, the sea-god Poseidon – known as Neptune to the Romans. Scholars now believe it is more likely to have been the temple of Hera or Zeus. It appears to have been modelled on the Greek motherland's Temple of Zeus at Olympia. Colonists from the city of Sybaris (on the south Italian coast's Gulf of Taranto) built it around 460BC, perhaps 30 years after settling in Paestum.

The excellent state of preservation of this masterpiece of the classical era gives a complete idea of what most Greek temples were like. Solidly planted on its platform, the temple has retained its architrave, entablature, frieze of metopes and triglyphs, and a pediment supported by a Doric peristyle of six columns on the front and 14 columns along the sides. It measures 20m (66ft) by 60m (197ft). In the interior, a *pronaos* (vestibule) precedes a vast *cella* (central chamber), with the nave separated from its two side aisles by rows of double columns. Placed at the front of the temple are altars for the ritual sacrifice of animals, and for the placing of fruit and other offerings.

The popularity of Paestum on the Grand Tour undertaken by British and American gentlemen in the 18th and 19th centuries was such that elements from sketches of the Temple of Neptune showed up on the facades of banks, museums and plantation mansions from London to Louisville.

32s Via Magna Grecia 87, Paestum 082 881 1016 Daily 9 to one hour before sunset; Museum: daily 9–7 (closed 1st and 3rd Mon of the month) Site moderate; site and museum expensive Café (€) From Salerno (Piazza della Concordia) Paestum (from Salerno) Via Magna Grecia 887 082 881 1016

9 Villa dei Misteri, Pompei

www.pompeiisites.org

One of the finest of Pompei's villas, the Villa dei Misteri is famous for its cycle of frescoes of life-size figures enacting the rituals of the Dionysiac cult.

The Villa of the Mysteries stands outside the Porta Ercolano, the ancient city gate to Herculaneum, at the end of Via dei Sepolcri, a street lined with the monumental tombs of prominent Pompeian citizens. The villa was a grand country house, the residence of a prosperous gentleman farmer and wine-grower. It was probably built in the 2nd century BC, renovated around 60BC and then again just before the eruption of Vesuvius in AD79. It was built on ground sloping down to the sea, then much closer than it is today, with terraces and porticoes offering fine views. Frescoes show the patrician family's taste for the good life in the fashionable Hellenistic manner.

Through the east entrance, visitors reached the villa's spacious peristyle or colonnaded courtyard. Kitchens are off to the south and the *torcularium* (room for wine production) lies to the north. Two massive wooden winepresses (one reconstructed with a carved ram's head)

crushed out the last juices of the trampled grapes into terracotta jars set in the floor.

Residential quarters are grouped around an atrium west of the peristyle. The bedrooms *(cubicula)* are enhanced by *trompe l'oeil* frescoes of elegant arched porticoes opening out to gardens and other buildings. An open living room *(tablinum)* has delicately detailed frescoes of Egyptian deities painted on a dramatic black background. The dining room *(triclinium)* is decorated on three sides with the magnificent fresco-cycle that gives the villa its name: ten richly coloured scenes of a young bride's initiation into the Dionysiac mysteries – a sensual cult much appreciated in the wine-growing region of Campania.

29q Via dei Sepolcri, Pompei Scavi
Zona Archeologica 081 857 5403
Apr–Oct daily 8:30–7:30 (last entry 6); Nov–Mar 8:30–5 (last entry 3:30). Closed 1 Jan, Easter Mon, 15 Aug, 25 Dec
Expensive, ticket includes main site and Villa dei Misteri. Joint ticket available, for entry to five sites, including Herculaneum
English-language tours; multi-language audio guides Cafeteria (€) Pompei–Scavi (Villa dei Misteri)
Via Sacra 1 081 850 8451

10 Villa Rufolo, Ravello

With their view of the Amalfi Coast, the gardens of this exquisite complex of 13th-century buildings inspired both writer Boccaccio and composer Wagner.

Opposite the Duomo, a medieval square tower stands at the entrance to one of the most enchanting villas in all southern Italy. The buildings, dating back to the 13th and 14th centuries, rise on hillside terraces overlooking the sea. Arabic influence is apparent in the ornate architecture, especially in the intertwining pointed arches of the cloister-like courtyard. The villa's chapel has an interesting antiquarium of ancient Roman and medieval sarcophagi, funeral urns and architectural fragments.

With their umbrella pines and majestic cypresses, the gardens are heavy with the fragrance of exotic plants. From the terrace, look down over the domes of Ravello's little 13th-century Annunziata church to the coastal village of Atrani. The villa has attracted popes and kings, and it was in these gardens that Giovanni Boccaccio walked with his beloved Fiammetta when escaping from his office job in Naples in 1330. He devoted one of his famous stories in *The Decameron* to the villa's wealthy owner, Landolfo Rufolo, who resorted to piracy to break the competition of merchants from Genoa.

Over 500 years later, German composer Richard Wagner took the Villa Rufolo's gardens as his model for the Garden of Klingsor in his last opera, *Parsifal*, a solemn religious drama begun here in 1877 and produced at Bayreuth in 1882. Ravello celebrates

this inspiration every summer with an open-air festival of Wagner's and other composers' music performed in the Rufolo gardens.

29q Piazza Duomo 1, Ravello 089 857 657 Daily 9 to sunset Moderate Café/restaurant (€–€€) SITA bus once daily from Naples, half-hourly from Amalfi 6am–9pm Festival Musicale di Ravello 089 858 149; www.ravellofestival.com
Via Roma 18 bis 089 857 096

Best things to do

Best things to take home

Shop for a bottle of *limoncello*, a *digestivo* made from lemons. Sip it chilled after dinner, or try the *crema di limoncello*, an unctuously smooth and creamy version. It's made in Sorrento, along the Amalfi coast and on Capri, with each producer claiming his own is the only real thing.

Pop into one of the tiny sandal shops in Naples and down the coast, where you can order a pair of super-light summer sandals, designed and made especially for you in a couple of days.

Acquire a string of brilliantly coloured *peperoncini*, fiery hot dried chillies for spicing up pasta sauces. Look for the hottest of the hot, known by the locals as *viagra naturale*.

Pick up shirts and dresses made for the *gran'caldo*, the great summer heat, in lightest linen and cotton in a rainbow of vibrant colours.

Head for one of the local perfume manufacturers, where you'll find soap, cleansers, bath oils and candles whose scents recall the wild flowers, herbs and lemons of the Naples area.

Stock up on herbs and spices at local markets, or drop into a specialist coffee store for an espresso maker and the potent, high-roast coffee loved by Neapolitans.

Indulge in high-fashion designer-name purchasing or browsing in the big-name stores in Naples or on Capri – everything from Ferragamo and Gucci to Bulgari and Missoni.

Buy calendars for next year – on sale from April – or a beautiful coffee-table art book to remind you of the treasures and scenic beauty of Naples and the coast.

Search a ceramic store for something that appeals among the bright, hand-decorated plates, platters, bowls and jugs in colours that sing.

Shop for *artigianata* – craftwork local to Naples and around. Good buys include *presepi* (tiny crib figures), hand-woven baskets and stunning intarsia wood inlay work from Sorrento.

Good cafés and restaurants

La Caffettiera

Sit indoors in the tea room or on the fashionable terrace outside from where you can watch the smart people of the Chiaia quarter. Neopolitan pastries are served here, including the delicious *baba* cakes and crispy *sfogliatelle* pastry.

✉ Piazza dei Martiri 25, Naples ☎ 081 764 4243.

Gambrinus

Dating from 1860, this is Naples oldest café and something of an institution. Excellent for people-watching.

✉ Piazza Trieste e Trento, Naples ☎ 081 417 582.

Gran Caffè

Join the charming islanders for an apéritif on the terrace after your meal and fully appreciate this beatiful island.

✉ Piazzetta Umberto I, Capri ☎ 081 837 0388.

Intra Moenia

A funky café/bookshop that is great favourite with students and writers. The calming atmosphere provides a good bolt hole from the hectic street life outside

✉ Piazza Bellini 70, Naples ☎ 081 290 720.

O Parrucchiano

Nicknamed La Favorita, this Sorrento institution does a roaring trade all year round. The recommended dishes here are cannelloni, gnocchi and fish simply grilled with a little lemon.

✉ Corso Italia 71, Sorrento ☎ 081 878 1321

Pasticceria Andrea Pansa

Traditional, high-class café and *pasticceria* specializing in lemon confectionery. Sit outside and indulge in a *delizia al limone*, a snow-white mound of sponge and lemon cream that melts in the mouth.

✉ Piazza del Duomo 40, Amalfi ☎ 089 871 065

La Savardina da Edoardo

There is a lovely walk from Capri Town to this charming trattoria in a citrus garden. Try linguine in herbs, cherry tomatoes, garlic and fresh anchovy or raviloi with *caciotta* cheese.

✉ Via Lo Capo, Capri ☎ 081 837 6300

Scaturchio

Delicious pastries right on one of the city's most handsome squares. The *sfogliatelle* is superb.

✉ Piazza di San Domenico Maggiore 19, Naples ☎ 081 551 6944

Villa Brunella

Sample some the best cuisine Capri has to offer at this hotel's terrace restaurant with a romantic vista of Marina Piccola.

✉ Via Tragara 24, Capri ☎ 081 837 0122

La Zagara

Try the famous chocolate cake while you sit in the shade of the lemon trees.

✉ Via dei Mulini 6/8, Positano ☎ 089 875 964

Top activities

Canoeing

Hire a boat or canoe from Bagni Le Sirene Marina Piccola on Capri and explore the amazing grottoes that surround the island.
✉ Via Mulo 63, Capri ☎ 081 837 0221

Diving

With its rich aquatic wildlife and submerged Greek and Roman sites, the Bay of Naples and the Amalfi Coast are wonderful places to go diving; Sea Point Italy offer diving classes geared to all different levels supervized by a team of qualified instructors.
✉ Via Molo di Baia 14, Baia ☎ 081 868 8868; www.seapointitaly.it

Fishing

The Amalfi Coast is a better spot for fishing than the Bay of Naples. No licence is required for sea fishing from shore or boat.

Football

As far as religion goes, football comes just after, and for many just before, the Catholic church. In his heyday, taxis carried effigies of (now-disgraced) Argentine star Maradonna next to the

Madonna. You can see the Naples team, Napoli, play in the two-tiered San Paolo stadium.

✉ Piazzale Vincenzo Tecchio, Naples ☎ www.sscnapoli.it ? Tickets: Via Francesco Galeota 19 (☎ 081 593 40001; www.calcionapoli1926.it)

Hot springs

Pay a visit to Ischia's Nuove Terme Comunale (public spa facilities) to indulge in thermal treatments, mudbaths and massage.

✉ Via delle Terme, Ischia ☎ 081 984 376

Mountain-biking

Many of the Amalfi Coast's resorts hire bicycles for you to explore the back country.

Mountaineering

One of the most exhilarating experiences is climbing Vesuvius or the Lattari mountains behind Amalfi. If you fancy a trekking or climbing excursion visit the website of the local Club Alpino Italiano branch.

✉ Via Trinita degli Spagnoli 41, Naples ☎ www.cainapoli.it

Sailing

The best sailing is from Posíllipo harbour in Naples, or Positano, Amalfi, Capri and Ischia. The Bay of Naples' major sporting event is Capri's international regatta held in May. Regional regattas may be held in summer at the major Amalfi Coast resorts – and Naples, too. For details, check with the tourist information offices at Positano, Amalfi and Naples.

Walking

Self-guided or accompanied walking tours on the Amalfi Coast and the Sorrento peninsula are organized by ATG-Oxford.

✉ 69–71 Banbury Road, Oxford ☎ 01865 315678 (brochure line 01865 315665); www.atg-oxford.co.uk

a walk from Piazza Dante to Forcella

Walk by way of Piazza Bellini from Via dei Tribunali's aristocratic *palazzi*, churches and markets to the workshops of Forcella. Visit the treasures of San Gregorio Armeno (➤ 90–91), San Lorenzo Maggiore (➤ 100), the Duomo (➤ 92) and Pio Monte della Misericordia (➤ 98).

After a quick peek at the narrow streets of the Quartieri Spagnoli (Spanish Quarter) west of the Via Toledo off Piazza Dante, take the arched gateway left off the piazza to cut through Via Port'Alba to Piazza Bellini.

Luigi Vanvitelli designed Piazza Dante's monumental crescent in 1757 – now embracing a 19th-century statue of Dante. Students throng the bookshops in the Via Port'Alba arcade and the café terraces of Piazza Bellini, overlooking remains of the ancient Greek city walls (4th century BC).

From the southeast corner of Piazza Bellini, take Via San Pietro a Maiella and cross Piazza Miraglia to continue along Via dei Tribunali, with short digressions to churches right on Via San Gregorio Armeno, left on Via Duomo.

San Pietro a Maiella convent houses the Conservatorio di Musica. Via dei Tribunali is the central of three ancient *decumanus* streets, crossing the Greek agora and Roman forum on Piazza San Gaetano. Fruit, vegetable, fish and meat markets like those in today's arcades have been here for 2,500 years.

Back on Via dei Tribunali, turn right at the church of Santa Maria della Pace on Via della Pace. Cross Via Vicaria Vecchia to enter Via Forcella forking to the right across Piazza Calenda to Corso Umberto I.

The names of the side streets here testify to the time-honoured crafts of bustling Forcella: *intagliatori* (wood-carvers), *candelari* (chandlers), *armaioli* (gunsmiths) and *chiavettieri* (locksmiths).

Distance 2km (1.2 miles)
Time 2–3 hours, with visits to churches and street markets
Start point Piazza Dante ✚ 7F Ⓜ Dante 🚌 C63, R4
End point Forcella ✚ 10F 🚌 R2 on Corso Umberto I
Lunch Pizzeria di Matteo, a monument in itself (€)
✉ Via dei Tribunali 94 ☎ 081 455 262

Stunning views

Naples and the harbour from Capodimonte (➤ 44–45).

Spaccanapoli from Certosa di San Martino (➤ 89).

Bay of Naples from Vesuvius (➤ 40–41).

Vesuvius from Santa Lucia (➤ 102).

Capri's Faraglioni rocks from Parco Augusto (➤ 117).

Island of Capri from Sorrento cliffs (➤ 130).

Pompei's amphitheatre from the top seats, facing Vesuvius (➤ 72).

Along the Amalfi Coast from Vietri near Salerno (➤ 143).

Amalfi from the gardens of Ravello's Villa Rufolo (➤ 54–55).

Across the Bay of Naples from the Villa Comunale in Sorrento (➤ 130).

Places to take the children

Beaches

Ischia's north coast offers the best sandy beaches for family swimming and water sports. A popular beach for tourists and locals on the south coast is the Spiaggia Grande. Positano (➤ 46–47) has several beaches and coves, fairly close to the harbour. La Porta has the added attraction of Stone Age cave dwellings to explore. To reach Capri's best beaches, you have to take a boat.

Boat cruises

The whole family can enjoy exploring the grottoes on boat cruises around Capri and along the rugged Amalfi Coast, particularly the Grotta Azzurra (➤ 38–39) and Grotta di Smeralda (➤ 139).

Museo di Capodimonte

Even if you cannot coax them inside the museum (➤ 44–45), children enjoy the pretty palace gardens, so take a picnic – and a football which, despite signposts to the contrary, is a favourite pastime there.

Christmas figurines

The Neapolitan art of modelling miniature figures for *presepi* (Christmas mangers) began 600 years ago, inspired by Francis of

Assisi's live re-enactment of the scene at Greccio in 1223. The tradition thrives all year round in workshops around Via San Gregorio Armeno. Children will love to see them at work at Certosa di San Martino (► 89), although the most famous workshop is Ferrigno (✉ Via San Gregorio Armeno 55 ☎ 081 580 0167).

Eating out

How can you go wrong in a place that makes the best pizza in the world? In the same restaurant that serves something more sophisticated to their parents, kids can have their favourite *quattro stagione*, or discover a pocket *calzone* (actually 'trousers') pizza they can eat with both fists. And then there's the ice-cream!

Edenlandia

This huge funfair is out at Mostra d'Oltremare trade fairgrounds to the west of Mergellina.

✉ Viale Kennedy 76 ☎ 081 239 4090; www.edenlandia.it 🚆 Ferrovia Cumana (Montesanto) to Edenlandia or ANM buses C2, C3 or 152

Monte Vesuvio

Visiting Vesuvius (Monte Vesuvio, ► 40–41), and trekking the last stretch to the crater, is quite an adventure for older children.

Ospedale delle Bambole

This tiny dolls' hospital in the heart of Spaccanapoli is one of the city's most enchanting shops, and children are captivated by it.

✉ Via San Biagio dei Librai 81 ☎ 081 563 4744

Pompei

Try not to overdo it when taking children to the region's best archaeological sites: Pompei (► 126–129) is fine for a couple of hours, but take a good break for lunch. Concentrate on the houses and shops rather than the monuments, though it's fun to test the amphitheatre for its acoustics.

Naples churches

Chiesa di San Gregorio Armeno
Richly decorated, the church has a fascinating history and boasts beautiful works of art, tranquil cloisters, two organs, and a patron saint who works miracles (➤ 90–91).

Gesù Nuovo
This rather grim grey ashlar facade conceals a wealth of baroque riches, Neapolitan art and memories of a modern saint (➤ 95).

San Domenico Maggiore
A large church standing in one of the busiest piazzas in Naples, with many beautiful works of art (➤ 98–99).

San Giacomo degli Spagnoli
Built in 1540, this fascinating small church reflects the Spanish occupation of the city, and contains the 16th-century tombs of Spanish nobles. To the rear of the altar is the elaborate marble tomb of Don Pedro de Toledo, who built the church.
✉ Piazza Municipio ☎ 081 552 3759 ⏲ Tue–Sat 7:30–11, Sun 11–2 🚌 C22, C25, E5, R2, R3

San Giovanni a Carbonara
Intended to house the tombs of the Angevin rulers in the 15th century, this 14th-century chapel is one of the most historically important in Naples. Entry is via a steep flight of steps and inside you will find some magnificent monuments. Most notable is the one high above the altar of King Ladislas. Under the altar is a doorway to the lovely round chapel.
✉ Via San Giovanni a Carbonara 5 ☎ 081 295 873 ⏲ Mon–Sat 9:30–1 🚇 Piazza Cavour 🚌 110, E1

San Lorenzo Maggiore
An impressive Gothic church with interesting monuments and a fascinating excavation site underneath (➤ 100).

San Paolo Maggiore
On the site of a Roman temple; pillars can still be seen on the church facade. An impressive staircase leads to the entrance. The huge interior has been restored, and there are some lovely frescoes, and paintings by Stazione and Solimena.
✉ Via dei Tribunali ☎ 081 454 048 ⏲ Mon–Sat 9–12
Ⓜ Dante 🚌 E1, R2

Santa Chiara
Rising from the ashes of war, this beautiful church and its enchanting cloisters emanate peace and simplicity (➤ 100–101).

Santa Maria del Carmine
With the tallest campanile in the city it is impossible to overlook this church (➤ 103).

Santa Maria della Sanità
Built in 1613, this spacious church is in the pattern of a Greek cross; in the centre is a large dome supported by 24 columns. But the real interest of this formal church lies beneath in the catacombs, where there are traces of frescoes dating back to the fifth century and some gruesome remains from the 17th century, when the skulls were set into the wall – visits are by guided tour.
✉ Via Sanità 124 ☎ 081 544 1305 ⏲ Mon–Sat 8:30–12:30, Sun 8:30–1:30 🚌 47, 182, C51, C52, C64

Pompei ruins

Amphitheatre

Built in the second century BC – one of the oldest of its kind in existence – the theatre held 5,000 people.

✉ Piazzale Anfiteatro

Forum

The oldest part of Pompei, dating from at least the second century. Standing at the highest point, the forum was the heart of political and commercial life.

✉ Via Marina

House of Julia Felix

Home of a wealthy Pompei resident, this large house was rented out as homes and shops, and contained public baths.

✉ Via dell'Abbondanza

House of the Citarista

Two houses once stood here that surrounded many courtyards. The name comes from a statue of Apollo playing a lyre, now in the Museo Archeologico in Naples.

✉ Via Stabiana

House of the Faun

The wealth bestowed on this important private residence is apparent in the beautiful wall paintings and the mosaic tiles.

✉ Via della Fortuna

House of the Golden Cupids

The bedroom is the main attraction here with its amazing gold cupids, after which the house is named. Although modest in size, the house has some interesting wall paintings and a restored garden with a pool and sculptures.

✉ Vicolo dei Vetti

House of the Mysteries

Here you will find the best-preserved frescoes in Pompei, which tell the story of a young bride being initiated into the cult of Dionysus. The house was built as an urban villa, but was converted into a country residence around 60BC.

✉ Via delle Tombe

House of the Vetii

Owned by wealthy merchants, the house has many well-preserved murals and a lovely garden. The most popular attraction, however, is the room that features famous erotic paintings.

✉ Vicolo dei Vetii

Via dell'Abbondanza

As you walk down this street lined with shops, inns and private houses, you can easily imagine people going about their daily life. At the end of the road is the public baths and a brothel.

Via delle Tombe

This solemn road is lined with tombs carrying inscriptions of the main families of the city; a Roman custom considered a sign of respect. Look for the wheel tracks still indented into the road.

Piazzas and streets

Piazza Bellini, Naples

Always thronged with people, this lively piazza is the most fashionable spot in the city. Cafés and restaurants and some interesting buildings surround a statue of the composer Vincenzo Bellini looking down on excavations of the old city walls.

Piazza Dante, Naples

Redesigned in the 18th century to accommodate the palace of King Charles III, this large, elegant piazza retains its stately aura. The centrepiece is a statue of Dante.

Piazza del Duomo, Amalfi

Amalfi offers, on Piazza del Duomo, a delightfully relaxed atmosphere on the terraces of cafés, ice-cream parlours and restaurants looking across to the cathedral's noble stairway.

Piazza del Plebiscito, Naples

The neoclassical harmony of this airy piazza, enclosed in a gracefully curving colonnade, was originally planned in 1810 in secular style. At the centre of the colonnade is the domed Chiesa di San Francesco di Paola. The piazza's two equestrian statues are of Ferdinand and Charles III of Bourbon.

Piazza Umberto I, Capri

The island's capital has at its centre one of the Mediterranean's most fashionable meeting places, Piazza Umberto I, better known as the Piazzetta, more courtyard than square. Its cafés look across to a sturdy clock tower and the quaint Moorish-baroque Santo Stefano church.

Spaccanapoli, Naples

The heart of Naples, this historic road encapsulates a wealth of art and architecture, shops, restaurants and bars (► 48–49).

Via Anticagliai, Naples
This Roman road is interesting to explore for the remains of its origins. Note the arches across the road which used to link the bathhouse with the playhouse where Emperor Nero performed.

Via Scarlatti, Naples
Located in the smart area of Vomero hill, this pedestrianized street upholds the image with its classy shops and plane trees that line both sides. Take a break at one of the tempting cake and ice-cream options during a fun afternoon of retail therapy.

Via Toledo, Naples
Glance above the shop fronts and you will see the facades of many historic *palazzi* in this mostly pedestrianized shopping street on the edge of the Quartieri Spagnoli. When built in the 16th century, it was one of Europe's most elegant streets.

Great ice-cream

Andrea Pansa

Andrea Pansa has been providing amazing ice-creams and totally delicious white chocolate profiteroles for years.

✉ Piazza Duomo 40, Amalfi ☎ 089 871 065

Bilancione

There are usually long seafront queues for the city's most popular ice-cream parlour. The hazelnut *(nocciola)* has won a Golden Cone *(Cona d'Oro)* in the world ice-cream championships. The exquisite fresh fruit flavours change with the seasons.

✉ Via Posillipo 238/6, Naples ☎ 081 769 1923

Chocolate

Ultra-modern and sleek, Chocolate epitomizes the modern *gelato* scene with flavours such as *canella* (cinnamon) and *caramello argentino* (caramel); try the *semifreddi*, cups filled with a cross between ice cream and mousse.

✉ Piazza Rodinò 26, Chiaia, Naples ☎ 081 794 4140

Davide

Unashamedly calls itself *Il Gelato* (The Ice-cream). There's an astonishing choice of 60 flavours – try the summer fruit ices

such as *lampone* (raspberry), *pesca* (peach) and *melone* (melon).
✉ Via Padre Reginaldo Giuiani 39, Sorrento ☎ 081 807 2092

Fantasia Gelati
Exotic combinations of ice-cream are sold here and at the other branches on Via Toledo and Via Cilea.
✉ Piazza Vanvitelli 22, Naples ☎ 081 578 8383

Otranto
For the creamiest concoctions in 30 ever-changing flavours near Certosa di San Martino.
✉ Via Scarlatti 78, Naples ☎ 081 558 7498

Remy Gelo
Choose from over 30 flavours of ice-cream, as well as many types of granita and frozen yoghurts, plus ice-cream pastries.
✉ Via Ferdinando Galiani 29, Naples ☎ 081 668 480

Scialapopolo
A tiny kiosk serving some of the best ice cream and *granite* on the island – try the refreshing *granita al limone* on a hot day.
✉ Via Vittorio Emanuele 55, Capri ☎ 081 837 0558 🕐 Closed Nov–Mar

La Scimmia
A pioneer on Naples' gelati scene (it's existed for over 60 years), La Scimmia made its name with classic banana, but it also does great *crema torrone* (nougat) and pistachio.
✉ Piazza Carità 4 (off Via Toledo), Naples ☎ 081 552 0272

La Zagara
Superb ice-cream and pastries in a charming lemon grove; the main attraction is *granita* (iced drinks) of strawberry, lemon, almond and even fig.
✉ Via dei Mulini 6/8, Positano ☎ 089 875 964

Naples museums and galleries

Certosa di San Martino
This glorious building with superb views and containing a wonderful collection of art is a highlight of a visit to Naples (► 89).

Città della Scienza
This science museum has explanations in English and Italian. The planetarium and hands-on exhibits will keep children entertained.
✉ Via Coroglio 104 ☎ 081 372 3728; www.cittadellascienza.it 🕔 Tue–Sat 9–5, Sun 10–7; closed Aug ✋ Moderate 🍴 Café 🚌 C9, C10

Madre
This contemporary art museum and exhibition space has works by artists such as Damien Hirst, Jeff Koons and Anish Kapoor hanging

alongside pieces by contemporary Italian artists such as Lucio Fontana and Pietro Manzoni. The upper floors are devoted to temporary exhibitions.

✉ Via Settembrini 79 ☎ 081 562 4561 or 081 1931 3016; www.museomadre.it ⏲ Mon–Fri 10–9, Sat–Sun 10am–midnight
💰 Expensive 🍴 Café and restaurant 🚌 E1

Museo Archeologico Nazionale

A well organized museum packed with priceless objects that will give you a good insight into the ruins of Pompei (➤ 42–43).

Museo di Capodimonte

Appreciate some of the best Italian art and panoramic views at this beautiful palace set on a hill (➤ 44–45).

Museo del Mare

Naples' Naval Institute runs this splendidly traditional museum devoted to all things nautical. The accent is on the development of maritime technology, with good displays of charts and instruments down the centuries, as well as fine model ships of all descriptions.

✉ Via Pozzuoli 5 ☎ 081 617 3749; www.museodelmarenapoli.it
⏲ Mon–Sat 9–1, 3–7 💰 Free 🚌 152

Museo Villa Pignatelli

A noble neoclassical Doric-columned villa, built in 1826, with beautiful gardens. The villa is home to the Banco di Napoli art collection, which includes Francesco Guarino's *St George* (c1650) and some superb 18th- and 19th-century landscapes.

✉ Riviera di Chiaia 200 ☎ 081 761 2356 ⏲ Wed–Mon 8:30–1:30
💰 Inexpensive 🚌 C12, C18

Palazzo Reale

The seat of power in Naples for three centuries, this elaborate royal palace held one of the most important courts in Europe (➤ 96–97).

Exploring

Historic, frenetic yet elegant, if a little frayed around the edges, Naples is southern Italy's main city, set on a wide bay, with Vesuvius looming to the south and the Sorrento and Amalfi coastlines little more than an hour away. Ever since the Grand Tourists of the 18th and 19th centuries flocked here, it's been pulling in the crowds, and today it's once more high on the Italian hit list.

Visitors come for the baroque churches and Renaissance palaces, for the opera and the theatre, the good food and the colourful street life. They find a city that offers all this in abundance – top-class museums, a city centre that's been spruced up but manages to retain its chaotic charm, churches dripping with stucco and gilt, and a population that is one of Naples' richest assets. Whether you're in classy Chiaia or amid the frenzy of Via dei Tribunale, the people are perhaps the greatest stars of the show.

Naples

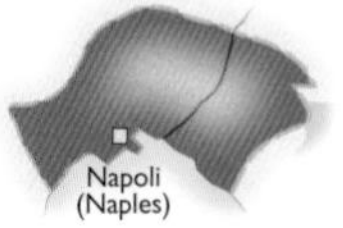

The city's *centro storico* (historic centre) keeps to the limits of the old Graeco–Roman town, much of it now a pedestrian zone. Almost all the major monuments are located in the narrow triangle formed by the Museo Archeologico, the Duomo (Cathedral) and Piazza del Plebiscito. It is all level going except for the hilltop Certosa di San Martino to the west and the Museo di Capodimonte to the north.

To tour the city in easy stages, it is a good idea to keep to three or four separate itineraries. Some like to start with an overall view of the city, from the terrace of the Certosa di San Martino or Castel Sant'Elmo. Others like to begin in the thick of it, with Spaccanapoli, which, with leisurely stops at the major sights, can occupy one or two full days. Similarly, it is possible to spend one or two days exploring the Via Tribunali, taking the circular walk beginning at Piazza Dante. Reserve half a day each for an unhurried tour of both the Museo di Capodimonte and Museo Archeologico.

A stroll down Via Toledo (also known as Via Roma) and around Via Chiaia provides a mixture of sightseeing and shopping, taking in both the fashionable boutiques and the Palazzo Reale and Castel Nuovo. Spare time, too, for the bourgeois Vomero area around the gardens of Villa Floridiana and the celebrated Santa Lucia district down by the harbour.

28p

CAPPELLA SANSEVERO

The mystery and beauty of its interior make this chapel one of the city's most attractive and intriguing baroque buildings. It is now a museum situated just behind Piazza San Domenico Maggiore (► 98–99). Built in 1590 as the Sangro family's private chapel, it became a mausoleum for the princes of Sansevero (Severo was a canonized 4th-century bishop of Naples). In the 18th century, the chapel was given its luminous artistic unity by Don Raimundo de'Sangro, leading figure of the Neapolitan Enlightenment, soldier, scientist, man of letters, Grand Master of the city's Freemasons and brilliant patron of the arts.

The Sansevero ceiling has a joyously coloured fresco, *Gloria del Paradiso* (1749) by Francesco Maria Russo, but the outstanding feature is the chapel's sculpture. Left and right of the arch leading to the high altar are Antonio Corradini's sensual *Pudicizia Veluta* (Veiled Modesty, a homage to Don Raimundo's mother) and Francesco Queirolo's *Disinganno* (Disillusion), an artistic *tour de force* of a man entangled in a net carved entirely in marble. The high altar has a magnificent Deposizione sculpted by Francesco Celebrano. At the centre of the chapel, transferred from the crypt, is Giuseppe Sanmartino's extraordinary *Cristo Velato* (Shrouded Body of Christ).

In addition to the chapel's mystic symbolism, male and female skeletons displayed in a lower chamber, complete with meticulously reconstructed arteries and organs, have provoked speculation about Don Raimundo dabbling in alchemy or black magic. A simpler explanation would be his scientific studies of anatomy and his status as a prominent Freemason.

www.museosansevero.it

8F Via Francesco de Sanctis 19 081 551 8470 Mon, Wed–Sat 10–5:40; Sun and public hols 10–1:10 Moderate Café, pizzeria, restaurant (€–€€), Via dei Tribunali 24, C57, R2

CAPODIMONTE, MUSEO DI

Best places to see, ➤ 44–45.

CASTEL NUOVO

The formidable seafront fortress is still known to Neapolitans as the Maschio Angioino (Anjou kings' castle keep), though only a chapel remains from the 13th-century castle. The present structure was built by Catalan architect Guillem Sagrera for Alfonso of Aragon two centuries later. Its entrance, a white two-tiered triumphal arch, is a Renaissance masterpiece by Pietro de Martino and Francesco Laurana. The frieze over the lower arch celebrates Alfonso's triumphant entry into Naples in 1443. Beneath the pediment's river gods, and topped by St Michael, the statues over the upper arch represent the Four Virtues (Goodness, Thought, Knowledge and Wisdom).

A staircase in the inner courtyard leads to Sagrera's splendid rib-vaulted Sala dei Baroni (Baronial Hall). The city council now meets where barons were once arrested – many killed on the spot – for conspiring against Alfonso's illegitimate son Ferrante. A Renaissance portal and a rose window have been added to the Anjou kings' Gothic Cappella Palatina (Palace Chapel). Restoration revealed, in the window embrasures, precious fragments of frescoes (1330) by Maso Bianco and his Florentine master, Giotto.

They now form part of the castle's Museo Civico (Civic Museum), along with sculpture by Laurana and Domenico Gagini, and Neapolitan frescoes and paintings from the 15th to 18th centuries.

20J Piazza Municipio 081 420 1241/1342 Mon–Sat 9–7. Closed 1 Jan, 1 May, 25 Dec Expensive Caffè Gambrinus (€€), good restaurants near by (€–€€) C25, R2, R3

CASTEL SANT'ELMO

The massive hilltop citadel, in the form of a six-pointed star, was built by the Spanish in 1537 with tufa stone extracted from its moat. For centuries it was a prison for heretics, revolutionaries and leaders of the Risorgimento movement for Italian unity. The ramparts have a fine view of the city and Bay of Naples.

17H Largo San Martino 1, Via Tito Angelini 081 578 4030 or 081 800 288 Thu–Tue 8:30–6:30 (times and prices may vary according to exhibitions). Closed 1 Jan, Good Fri, 1 May, 25 Dec Inexpensive
Cafés, restaurants (€–€€) around Vomero's Piazza Vanvitelli
Funicolare (cable-car) Piazzetta Fuga; metro: Piazza Vanvitelli V1

CERTOSA DI SAN MARTINO

The majestic Certosa di San Martino (Charterhouse of St Martin) is impressive both for its artistic masterpieces and for the grand terrace views of Naples and the harbour. Consecrated in 1368, the richly endowed monastery was expropriated 500 years later by the new Italian state, but preserved as a museum to present its treasures as a representative history of Neapolitan art. Expanding the original conception of Siena's Tino di Camaino, better known as a sculptor, 17th-century architect Cosimo Fanzago gave it its predominantly baroque appearance.

An atrium to the church, on the left of the main courtyard, has frescoes by Belisario Corenzio and Domenico Gargiulo of *Henry VIII's Persecution of English Carthusian Monks*. Striking a more triumphant note for the church's Gothic-vaulted nave, Giovanni Lanfranco's ceiling fresco depicts Christ's Ascension. Of the many chapels don't miss the Cappella di San Gennaro (first left), with paintings by Battistello Caracciolo and sculptures of the Evangelists by Antonio Vaccario. José Ribera's superb *Apostles' Communion* is in the presbytery, and his *Deposition* is on the high altar. See, too, the beautiful 16th-century inlaid walnut panelled wardrobes in the sacristy.

Worth a visit is the Quarto del Priore (Prior's Apartments), with a spiral staircase leading down to a garden. The Chiostro Grande (Great Cloister) has a handsome marble fountain in its charming four-square Renaissance arcaded garden. In the monastery kitchens is a popular display of 18th- and 19th-century *presepi* (Christmas mangers), crowded with lovingly carved shepherds, peasants, angels and animals surrounding the Holy Family.

17H · Piazzale San Martino 5 · 081 558 6408 · Thu–Tue 8:30–7:30 (times and prices vary according to exhibitions). Closed 1 Jan, Good Fri, 1 May, 25 Dec · Expensive · Cafés, restaurants (€–€€) around Vomero's Piazza Vanvitelli · Funicolare (cable-car) Montesanto; metro: Piazza Vanvitelli · V1 · Look for artists at work on figures for *presepi* (Christmas mangers)

CHIESA DI SAN GREGORIO ARMENO

With its distinctive belfry straddling the narrow Via San Gregorio Armeno, this opulent baroque church is part of a well-endowed convent dedicated to the saint who first took Christianity to Armenia. In 726, nuns fled here with his relics from the Byzantine iconoclastic turmoil in Constantinople. Originally an Eastern Orthodox edifice, the church was rebuilt in the 16th century to meet the demands of the Catholic Counter Reformation, notably with a unified nave and four lateral chapels. Flemish artists created the sumptuous coffered wooden ceiling, with its gilded panels and 16 paintings of martyred saints. In the cupola and on the western wall, Luca Giordano's frescoes (sadly damaged by the humidity) depict St Gregory's martyrdom and the transfer of his relics to Naples. Also in a chapel here, since 1864, are the much-venerated relics of St Patrizia, another refugee from Constantinople.

To the north of the belfry, the convent entrance is at the top of a long stairway. The convent's cloister garden is still beautifully kept, fragrant and shady with orange, lemon and mandarin trees. In the middle, Matteo Bottigliero's monumental marble fountain (1733) has exquisite statues of Christ's meeting with the Samaritan woman. In the convent rooms you'll find many opulent artworks, brought in by novice nuns from wealthy families.

The street outside forms the unofficial centre of Naples' thriving manufacture of traditional figurines for *presepi* (Christmas mangers). The workshops sell their carefully crafted wares – miniature shepherds, sheep, dogs, angels, butchers, bakers and pizza-chefs – all year round, but Via San Gregorio Armeno reaches a bustling crescendo during the Christmas market. *Presepi* can be seen in their most extravagant form at the museum of Certosa di San Martino (➤ 89).

9F Via San Gregorio Armeno 1 081 552 0186 Mon–Sat 9–12, Sun 9–1 Free
Cafés, restaurants (€–€€) Via dei Tribunali
Metro Piazza Cavour

DUOMO

Steeped in the city's long architectural and spiritual history, the Duomo remains the focus of Naples' celebrated miracle, the annual liquefaction of the blood of its patron saint, San Gennaro. The cathedral stands on a site that has been sacred since the Greeks built a temple here to Apollo.

Today's neo-Gothic facade (1905) attempts to recapture the medieval character of the Anjou kings' church, itself incorporating two 4th- and 5th-century Christian basilicas. Evidence of these older structures includes the temple's antique marble columns, the basilica's mosaics and frescoes, and the rib-vaulted chapels of the Angevin-Gothic church, along with the baroque art that followed.

The cathedral has kept its three original Gothic portals, with Tino di Camaino's 14th-century *Madonna and Child* sculpture over the main entrance. Inside, beneath the ornate 17th-century coffered ceiling, the lofty nave has columns taken from ancient Graeco–Roman buildings. In the left aisle, the 4th-century basilica of Santa Restituta has been transformed into a baroque chapel. To the right of the apse the baptistery has graphic mosaic fragments in its dome. Off the right transept is the 13th-century Cappella Minutolo, with mosaic paving, elegant groin vaulting and a monumental tomb with a gabled canopy over the altar.

Most spectacular of all is the Cappella del Tesoro di San Gennaro, a dazzling baroque chapel that attracts the faithful each May and September to see the saint's blood liquefy in phials kept behind the main altar, along with Gennaro's head. Others are content to admire the frescoes of Domenichino and Giovanni Lanfranco and Ribera's painting of San Gennaro emerging unscathed from a furnace.

9E Via Duomo 147 081 449 097 Mon–Sat 8:30–12:30, 4:30–7, Sun 8:30–1, 5–7. Closed during services Free Cafés, restaurants (€–€€) Via Duomo, Via dei Tribunali Metro Piazza Cavour R2

GALLERIA UMBERTO I

Among the many quarrels between Naples and Milan is that over who has the finest monumental glass-and-steel shopping gallery. Milan's Galleria Vittorio Emanuele was inaugurated first, in 1878, but Naples' grand neo-Renaissance Galleria Umberto I, built nine years later, may claim to be the more imposing architectural achievement. Replacing the whole neighbourhood of Santa Brigida, ravaged by the cholera epidemic of 1884, it was conceived by architect Antonio Curri as an affirmation of the new Italian state's modern spirit. It was a natural complement to the prestigious Teatro San Carlo (➤ 104–105) and Palazzo Reale (➤ 96–97). The soaring glass-and-steel dome is 57m (187ft) high,

above a central mosaic paving of the Zodiac, from which colonnades branch out, richly decorated with all the polychrome marble and allegorical Graeco–Roman sculptures a prosperous and rather ostentatious 19th-century bourgeoisie could wish for.

In the heyday of Naples' belle époque, this precursor of the modern shopping mall attracted high society to the city's smartest cafés, intimate theatres and fashion emporia. Today, the atmosphere is more subdued, but reputable jewellers and other traditional shops remain. Respectable citizens still gather here at that blessed early evening hour of the *passeggiata*, when Italians traditionally take a stroll to discuss the vital issues of the day – forthcoming marriages, football, politics, football, religion and football.

19J Main entrance on Via San Carlo Arcade open permanently, shops 9–1, 4–7 or 9 or 10–7:30. Closed Sun Free Cafés (€) R2

GESÙ NUOVO

At the west end of Spaccanapoli (➤ 48–49), on a piazza originally just outside the Graeco–Roman city walls, the Jesuits' main church is housed in the 15th-century palace of the Sanseverino princes. (An earlier church, the Gesù Vecchio, stands in the university grounds on Corso Umberto I.) Also on the square, the Guglia dell'Immacolata (Column of the Virgin Mary) replaced, in 1747, an equestrian statue of Spain's Philip V, destroyed by the people, who then had to pay for the Jesuits' lavishly ornate rococo obelisk. The church has kept the Renaissance palace's sober diamond-point embossed facade, adding only the three windows and baroque ornament to the main entrance. The exuberantly colourful interior makes a dramatic contrast. Notice, on the entrance wall, Francesco Solimena's biblical fresco of *Heliodorus Driven from the Temple* and in the left transept Cosimo Fanzago's statues of David and a despondent Jeremiah.

19G Piazza del Gesù Nuovo 2 081 557 8111 Daily 7–12:30, 4–7:30 Free Cafés, restaurants (€–€€) R1

MONTEOLIVETO, SANT' ANNA DEI LOMBARDI

Thanks to close ties between Naples' Aragonese court and the Medici and Este princes, Florentine and north Italian art treasures make this 15th-century church a true museum of Renaissance art. In the Cappella Piccolomini (first on the left), Antonio Rossellino designed the monumental tomb for Maria of Aragon and sculpted the altar's splendid nativity bas-relief (1475). In the Cappella Tolosa are glazed terracottas of the Evangelisti by the Della Robbia workshop. Benedetto da Maiano's charming marble relief of the Annunciazione (1489) is in the Curiale chapel. In the Sagrestia Vecchia (Old Sacristy), with its ceiling frescoes by Giorgio Vasari, is Guido Mazzoni's poignant terracotta statue of the Dead Christ.

19H Piazza Monteoliveto 44 081 551 3333 Mon–Fri 9:30–12 Free Cafés, restaurants (€–€€), Via Toledo, Spaccanapoli R1 Museum temporarily closed for restoration, telephone before visiting

MUSEO ARCHEOLOGICO NAZIONALE

Best places to see, ➤ 42–43.

PALAZZO REALE

What began as a palace for the Spanish monarchy came ultimately, with later additions and transformations, to symbolize the new kingdom of a united Italy. The vast palace complex has five facades, the main one being its entrance on Piazza del Plebiscito. Incorporating the Spanish viceroy's Palazzo Vecchio, Domenico Fontana designed the Palazzo Reale in a hurry, in 1600, to receive a royal

visit from Philip III of Spain, who then failed to turn up. Subsequently, it was the residence of Spanish and Austrian Habsburg viceroys, then the Bourbon and Italian Savoyard kings.

In the 18th century, Luigi Vanvitelli filled in alternate arches of the main facade's arcade with niches. A century later, Umberto I commissioned eight statues of the rulers of the kingdom to illustrate the course of Naples' history from the beginning to its annexation to a united Italy. They underline the fascinating variety of the rulers' origins: Roger of Normandy, Friedrich von Hohenstaufen, Charles d'Anjou, Alfonso I of Aragon, Charles V of Habsburg, Charles Bourbon, Joachim Murat of Napoleonic France and Vittorio Emanuele II of Savoy.

The interior's monumental marble staircase was given its present neo-classical appearance after a fire in 1837. Today's furnishings for the royal apartments , by no means all originals, reflect the style and tastes of the 17th to the 19th centuries. Two charming survivals of the 17th century are the Teatrino di Corte (Court Theatre) and Cappella Reale dedicata all'Assunta (Royal Assumption Chapel).

19K Piazza del Plebiscito 1 081 400 547, 848 800 288 Mon–Tue, Thu–Sun 9–8 (ticket office closed one hour earlier). Closed Wed, 1 Jan, Good Fri, 1 May, 25 Dec Moderate Caffè Gambrinus (€€), restaurants Via Toledo (€–€€) Piazza Amadeo C18, C19, R3

PIO MONTE DELLA MISERICORDIA

A supreme masterpiece of Italian painting rewards a visit to the church of the charitable institution, Monte della Misericordia, still active after 400 years. On the octagonal church's high altar, Caravaggio's *Opere di Misericordia (Works of Charity*, 1606) is one of the most important religious pictures of the 17th century. The Lombard painter uses his mastery of light and shade to illustrate seven acts of charity in one brilliantly grouped composite scene.

The characters come straight from the streets of Spaccanapoli: a grave-digger shrouding a corpse; an irritable girl giving her breast milk to an old man in prison; a tired pilgrim; a gentleman clothing a naked beggar; and even the angels accompanying the Madonna and Child look like Neapolitan street urchins.

Take a look, too, at the seven other altars, each devoted to one of the works of charity. The last (from the right) has a remarkable *Liberazione di San Pietro dal Carcere (Liberating St Peter from Prison)* by Battistello Caracciolo, a leading disciple of Caravaggio.

www.piomontedellamisericordia.it

9E Via dei Tribunali 253 081 446 944 Church and Picture Gallery: Thu–Tue 9–2. Closed Wed Near by (€–€€) Metro Piazza Cavour C57, R2

SAN DOMENICO MAGGIORE

With its café terraces, elegant palazzi and ornate baroque obelisk, the Piazza di San Domenico is one of the most attractive meeting places in the *centro storico.* Entered through the 16th-century marble portal in its fortress-like apse, the church of San Domenico Maggiore (1283) underwent extensive neo-Gothic restoration in the 19th century. Frescoes (1309) attributed to Pietro Cavallini were recently rediscovered in the Cappella Brancaccio (third right). Left of the nave, the Cappella dei Carafa has a clever *trompe-l'oeil* ceiling fresco of cherubs looking down at

a 16th-century *presepe* (Christmas manger). A mausoleum for the Aragon court, the church has 45 sarcophagi draped in rich silks and velvet on balconies in the sacristy (off the right aisle). Francesco Solimena's ceiling fresco celebrates the Dominicans' *Triumph of Faith Over Heresy* (1709). The Faculty of Theology at the Dominican monastery (closed to the public) attracted intellectuals such as Thomas of Aquinas and Giordano Bruno (burned alive in 1600).

8F Piazza San Domenico Maggiore 081 459 188 Mon–Sat 8:30–12, 4:30–7; Sun and public hols 9–1, 5–7 Free Cafés on piazza (€) R1

SAN LORENZO MAGGIORE

Behind an 18th-century façade is one of southern Italy's outstanding Gothic churches, built in 1266 for Naples' first Franciscan monks by Charles of Anjou. San Lorenzo Maggiore combines French Gothic pointed arches, clustered piers and rib vaulting in the apse and ambulatory with Italian Gothic in the nave's broad walls and truss-beamed ceiling. Among the ambulatory's monumental tombs, notice Tino di Camaino's exquisite shrine for Caterina d'Austria (1323). Neapolitan Giovanno da Nola sculpted the superb high altar (1530) portraying saints Lorenzo, Anthony and Francis of Assisi. **Excavations** in the courtyard have revealed the Graeco–Roman food market and treasury which once occupied the site.

9E Piazza San Gaetano 081 290 580 Mon–Sat 7:45am–7pm, Sun 7:45–1, 5:30–7 Free Cafés near by (€–€€) Metro Piazza Cavour

Excavations

Mon–Sat 9:30–5:30; Sun 9:30–1:30 Inexpensive

SANTA CHIARA AND CHIOSTRO DELLE CLARISSE

The 14th-century church of the Franciscan order of Clarissan nuns, also known because of their oath of poverty as the Poor Clares, is especially beloved for possessing one of the most enchanting cloisters in Italy. With its blind arcades and lofty buttresses, the church itself is quite austere, the facade of yellow tufa stone unadorned except for a rose window above a porch of three pointed arches. Begun in 1328, the free-standing campanile had two upper storeys added in the 16th century. Bombing in 1943 destroyed the church's rich baroque decoration, which had been added in the 18th century, and reconstruction

restored the original, more sober Gothic style. Among the artworks that survived are monumental tombs by Tino di Camaino for Anjou Duke Charles of Calabria and his wife Marie de Valois, on the right wall of the presbytery. Most imposing of all, is the huge tomb of Robert of Anjou (1345) for which Florentine sculptors Giovanni and Pacio Bertini showed the king enthroned and also lying on his deathbed wearing a Franciscan habit.

Entered from outside, behind the church, the Chiostro delle Clarisse, an archaeological area and small museum offer a moment of tranquillity. In 1742, the architect Domenico Antonio Vaccaro divided the cloister garden into four with intersecting vine-shaded alleys. The low majolica-tiled walls and benches show charming scenes of the everyday life of 18th-century citizens. Octagonal pillars are decorated with intertwining vines and wisteria.

www.santachiara.info

20G Via Benedetto Croce, Via Santa Chiara 49/c 081 1957 5915
Mon–Sat 9:30–5:30, Sun 9:30–2 Moderate Near by (€–€€) C57
Guided and audio tours; occasional lectures and concerts

SANTA LUCIA

Thanks to the romantic songs of the fishermen and picturesque prints of its waterfront, Santa Lucia was once one of the most popular neighbourhoods in the city. The sailors' church of Santa Lucia a Mare is now set back from the sea since the harbour disappeared under landfill and new construction. The 20th-century promenade formed by Via Nazario Sauro and Via Partenope is lined with luxury hotels, restaurants and yacht clubs, along with a monumental 17th-century fountain, L'Immacolatella, attributed to Pietro Bernini.

On an island joined by a causeway to the Santa Lucia mainland is the Castel dell'Ovo (Castle of the Egg), a former military prison now used for temporary exhibitions. Claimed to be named after the Latin poet Virgil's magic egg, the name is more likely to be due to the castle's shape back in the 14th century.

19L Via Nazario Sauro, Via Partenope
Pizzerias and seafood restaurants (€–€€€)
R3

SANTA MARIA DEL CARMINE

The church belongs to a 12th-century Carmelite convent, and has been much changed over the years. The campanile, at 75m (210ft) the city's tallest, acquired its octagonal drum and majolica-tiled spire after a fire in the 17th century, commemorated by spectacular fireworks on the Carmelite feast on 16 July. The original Gothic design is submerged by the extravagant baroque and rococo décor of the 18th century. Neapolitans revere the 14th-century Byzantine icon of the *Madonna Bruna (Brown Madonna)* behind the altar and, from the same era, a miraculous wooden Crucifixion in a tabernacle suspended from the ceiling. During a military siege of 1439, the Christ figure is believed to have ducked its head to avoid a shell, thus losing only its crown of thorns.

23G Piazza del Carmine 2 081 201 196 Mon–Sat 7–12/12:30 (depending on Mass), 5–7:30, Sun and public hols 7–1:30 Free Cafés, restaurants (€–€€) in Piazza del Mercato R3

SPACCANAPOLI

Best places to see, ➤ 48–49.

TEATRO SAN CARLO

In 1737, Charles Bourbon commissioned this opera house, dedicated to his patron saint, to rival those of Venice and Rome. It was part of an ambitious building programme that included the Museo Archeologico Nazionale (➤ 42–43) and the palaces of Capodimonte (➤ 44–45) and Caserta. Coming at a time when Naples was the third largest city in Europe (after London and Paris), it proved to be a magnificent monument for the city's most popular artistic expression, the *bel canto*.

Building contractor-cum-impresario Angelo Carasale completed the work in just 300 days, carrying out Giovanni Antonio Medrano's opulent design in gold, silver and blue, the colours of the Bourbon royal household. To give the royal guests easy access to the theatre, it was built on to the Palazzo Reale. The backdrop could originally be opened out on to the palace gardens. With its 184 boxes arranged in six tiers, the San Carlo still seats an audience of 3,000, making it one of Europe's largest opera houses.

In 1810, in keeping with the French taste of the time, Napoleon's Joachim Murat had Tuscan architect Antonio Niccolini add a new neoclassical facade. Destroyed by fire six years later, it was faithfully rebuilt by Niccolini for the Bourbon King Ferdinand. Composers Rossini and Donizetti both wrote and conducted operas for the San Carlo, and in 1835 Donizetti directed the world première of his hyper-romantic tragedy, *Lucia di Lammermoor*. The guided tour will show you the architecture, but only a performance can convey the essential fourth dimension, the fervent Neapolitan audience.

www.teatrosancarlo.it

19K Via San Carlo 98/f 081 553 4565, 393 955 3146 Opera season Nov–Jun Opera very expensive; recitals expensive; guided tours moderate Caffè Gambrinus (€€), restaurants near by (€€) C25, R2, R3 Daily tours outside rehearsal times; contact theatre bookshop or book online – appointment obligatory

VILLA FLORIDIANA

The villa and its handsome gardens, now one of Naples' most attractive public parks, were designed in 1819 by Antonio Niccollini as a summer *palazzina* for Ferdinand Bourbon's wife, Lucia Migliaccio, Duchess of Floridia. Amid groves of oak, pine and lemon trees the neoclassical villa houses the **Museo Nazionale della Ceramica 'Duca di Martina',** which has an impressive collection of European, Chinese and Japanese ceramics. Placido de Sangro, Duke of Martina, was in the 1880s a passionate collector of all manner of *objets d'art* picked up on his travels around Europe – glassware, coral, bronzes – but, above all, it is his porcelain and majolica that make this museum outstanding. It ranges from Spanish–Moorish to Italian Renaissance, from finest German Meissen to French Sèvres, including one delightful piece from the Rambouillet palace dairy, a cup of unmistakable shape known as *Le sein de la Reine* (the Queen's Breast), without identifying the queen.

15J Via Domenico Cimarosa 77 081 578 8418 Villa: Wed–Mon 8:30–1:30. Gardens: daily 8:30–dusk Villa: inexpensive. Gardens: free Cafés and restaurants near by (€–€€) Metro Piazza Vanvitelli, Funicolare (cable-car) di Chiaia

Museo Nazionale della Ceramica 'Duca di Martina'

081 578 8418 Wed–Mon 8:30–2, but hours and prices may vary according to temporary exhibitions

HOTELS

Canada (€–€€)
Overlooking Mergellina harbour, very simple but clean, air-conditioned three-star accommodation; eight rooms with tiny baths. Convenient for hydrofoil to Capri.
✉ Via Mergellina 43 ☎ 081 680 952 Mergellina

Donnalbina 7 (€)
Twenty-first-century style is showcased in the airy and minimalist bedrooms of this excellent value and upmarket B&B. Rooms are spacious and it's set on a quiet street within easy reach of the *centro storico*. Breakfast is served in your room; WiFi access.
✉ Via Donnalbina 7 ☎ 081 1956 7817; www.donnalbina7.it 201, C57, R1, R2, R4

Excelsior (€€€)
A grand hotel; magnificent roof-garden view of Castel dell'Ovo.
✉ Via Partenope 48 ☎ 081 764 0111; www.excelsior.it 3

Hotel San Marco (€–€€)
Well placed for the main sights and land and sea transport, this good-value hotel offers well-sized rooms, functionally equipped bathrooms and friendly service. Double glazing and air-conditioning keep out the noise and heat, and the hotel has its own restaurant.
✉ Calata San Marco 26 ☎ 081 552 0338; www.sanmarcohotelnapoli.it R1, R2, R3, R4

Pinto Storey (€€)
Fashionable location behind Villa Pignatelli. Rooms tastefully furnished; impeccable bedlinen and bathrooms; friendly service.
✉ Via Giuseppe Martucci 72 ☎ 081 681 260; www.pintostorey.it R3

Rex (€€)
Rex is in a restored *palazzo* that has original ceiling paintings and art nouveau decor. Bright, colourful rooms, double-glazed and air-conditioned.
✉ Via Palepoli 12 ☎ 081 764 9389; www.hotel-rex.it R3

Santa Lucia (€€€)
Renovated neoclassical seafront hotel. Elegant, spacious and comfortable rooms. Breakfast buffet a major attraction.
✉ Via Partenope 46 ☎ 081 764 0666; www.thi.it/hotels/grand-hotel-santa-lucia 🚌 R3

Vesuvio (€€€)
Ultimate luxury hotel. Opulently furnished rooms; bay view. Enrico Caruso left his name on the most luxurious suite, the rooftop restaurant, and a pasta dish.
✉ Via Partenope ☎ 081 764 004; www.vesuvio.it 🚌 R3

Villa Capodimonte (€€€)
A modern but stylishly decorated establishment in a tranquil hillside location near Capodimonte Museum and park. Terrace restaurant.
✉ Via Moiariello 66 ☎ 081 459 000; www.villacapodimonte.it 🚌 110

RESTAURANTS

La Bersagliera (€€)
This historic restaurant, founded in 1919, has drawn politicians, artists and actors over the years, and still pleases with its classic Neapolitan cooking and wonderful atmosphere. All pasta is home-made and the fish is fresh off the boats; try the fish and leave room for a rum baba or traditional pastry for dessert.
✉ Borgo Marinari 10 ☎ 081 764 6016 🕓 Closed Tue and 2 weeks in Jan 🚌 R3, 140

Brandi (€–€€)
Having created the flagship Pizza Margherita in 1889 (► 13), this venerable pizzeria still attracts crowds. Try, too, *pizza all'ortolana* (garden vegetables) or *pescatora* (seafood). Delicious rum baba.
✉ Salita Sant'Anna di Palazzo 1 (behind Piazza Trieste e Trento) ☎ 081 416 928 🕓 Closed three days in mid-Aug 🚌 R2, R3

La Caffettiera
See page 60.

Cantina della Sapienza (€)
There are six menu combinations on offer at this cheap but delicious budget eating house near the Museo Nazionale. Try the *pasta al ragù* (spaghetti with meat sauce) or the sublime *parmigiano di melanzane* (baked aubergine) and wash it down with robust *vino locale.*
✉ Via della Sapienza 40 ☎ 081 459 078 🕓 Lunch only; closed Sun 🚌 C57, R4

La Cantinella (€€€)
Elegant address near big Santa Lucia hotels. Exquisite service, fresh seafood and exceptional wine cellar attract Naples' high society. Seafood pasta *(pappardelle agli scampi* and *tagliatelle Santa Lucia)* and monkfish in seafood sauce *(rana pescatrice)* are house specialities. Pastry chef does wonders with citrus fruit.
✉ Via Cuma 42 ☎ 081 764 8684 🕓 Closed Sun, mid-Aug 🚌 R3

La Chiacchierata (€€)
Family trattoria near Piazza del Plebiscito, with Mamma Anna cooking and checking everybody is happy. Robust cuisine, lusty vegetable soups. Daily change of menu, so let Anna choose for you. *Chiacchierata* means 'chat'.
✉ Piazzetta Matilde Serao 37 ☎ 081 411 465 🕓 Mon–Thu lunch only, Fri, lunch and dinner, Sat lunch only. Closed Sun and Aug 🚌 C22, C25, R2

Ciro a Santa Brigida (€€–€€€)
Run by the Pace family for over 100 years. Highest quality; subtle antipasti, old-fashioned *o pignatiello de vavella* (shellfish soup), seafood or vegetable pasta, and *pizza d'oro*, with whole cherry tomatoes.
✉ Via Santa Brigida 71, near Galleria Umberto I ☎ 081 552 4072 🕓 Closed Sun in summer 🚌 C25, R2

Don Salvatore (€€)
There are good-value set menus featuring Neapolitan specialities at this long-established restaurant in Mergellina. The antipasti are the highlight – try *polpo ai carciofi* (squid with artichokes) or

cecinielle (tiny fish patties) before moving on to home-made pasta or a fish or meat *secondo*. Great wine list.
✉ Via Mergellina 5 ☎ 081 681 817 ⊙ Closed Fri 🚌 140, C21, R3

Gambrinus
See page 60.

Giuseppone a Mare (€€–€€€)
One of Naples' top seafood restaurants with a grand bay view. Fresh fish, *tagliatelle al tartufo e asparagi* (truffles and asparagus), and *linguine al nero* (in squid ink). Good wines, rich choice of desserts.
✉ Via Ferdinando Russo 13, Capo Posillipo ☎ 081 575 6002 ⊙ Closed Sun dinner, Mon, Aug, Christmas 🚌 C21

Intra Moenia
See page 60.

Masaniello (€€)
In the stableblock of an old *palazzo* in *centro storico*, you can expect to find traditional Neapolitan dishes and great pizzas – especially with *rucola* (rocket) or *salsiccie* (sausage).
✉ Via Donnalbina 28 (behind Santa Maria La Nova church) ☎ 081 552 8863 ⊙ Closed Sun, few days Aug 🚌 R1

Di Matteo (€)
Di Matteo was Spaccanapoli's best-loved pizzeria long before President Bill Clinton visited in 1994, but it's even more crowded now. Expect to have to queue, but it's worth the wait. The Margherita is the purists' choice, commonly eaten Neapolitan-style *a libretto* (folded in two).
✉ Via dei Tribunali 94 ☎ 081 455 262 ⊙ Closed Sun, two weeks in Aug 🚇 Piazza Cavour

Mimì Alla Ferrovia (€€)
Grand family institution with a reputation for fine food, sufficient to make people miss trains. Simplicity and finesse combine in *pasta*

e fagioli (noodles and beans) and famous *linguine al Mimi* (scampi, shrimp, scallops) and plain fennel salad.
✉ Via Alfonsa d'Aragona 21 ☎ 081 553 8525 🕐 Closed Sun, week in mid-Aug Ⓜ Piazza Garibaldi

Osteria Castello (€)
A modest family trattoria in fashionable Chiaia serving fine *bucatini all'amatriciana* (pasta with ham and red bell-peppers), pepper steaks and good home-made desserts.
✉ Via Santa Teresa a Chiaia 38 ☎ 081 400 486 🕐 Closed Sun, Aug 🚌 R3

Il Pizzaiolo del Presidente (€)
Right in the heart of the *centro storico*, this classic pizzeria, turning out over 2,000 pizzas a day, serves a superb pizza margherita and a full range of *pizze* with other toppings. There are no frills, food arrives in a flash and the cool basement area is an oasis in the summer heat.
✉ Via dei Tribunali 120 ☎ 081 210 903 🕐 Closed Sun Ⓜ Cavour

Scaturchio
See page 61.

Taverna dell'Arte (€€)
With tasteful and romantic decor, this fine old trattoria in the *centro storico* serves typical Neapolitan dishes: *minestra maritata* soup, stuffed pork, a great variety of vegetables and local wines.
✉ Rampa San Giovanni Maggiore 1a ☎ 081 552 7558 🕐 Dinner only. Closed Sun 🚌 C25, R2

SHOPPING

Antiche Delizie
Wonderful delicatessen, with outstanding cheese, meats and wines.
✉ Via Pasquale Scura 14 ☎ 081 551 3088 🚌 24, 105, R1

Arte in Oro
Well-priced and beautiful replicas of classical Roman jewellery and

individualistic modern pieces are created by a highly skilled team. No credit cards.

Via Benedetto Croce 20 081 551 6980 R1, R2, R3, R4

Bowinkel

Wonderful collection of Naples prints, bronzes, fans, costumes.

Piazza dei Martiri 24 081 764 4344 R2, R3

Caso

Highly reputed for its antique jewels, vintage watches and delicate coralware.

Piazza San Domenico Maggiore 16 081 552 0108/551 6733

Coin

Excellent for one-stop shopping with a sophisticated range of goods.

Via Scarlatti 90–98 081 578 0111

Drogheria Santa Chiara

A splendid source of all things Neapolitan, from locally produced foods and wines to candles and ceramics – perfect take-home souvenirs and gifts.

Via Benedetto Croce 50 Dante E1, R1

Eddy Monetti

Two stores, one for men and one for women, are considered locally to offer the best there is for classic Neapolitan fashion, timeless and of superb quality. They have their own label and also sell Blumarine, Pucci and Ralph Lauren.

Via dei Mille 45 (menswear) 081 407 064 C25; funicular Chiaia
Piazzetta Santa Caterina 8 (womenswear) 081 403 229 C25

Feltrinelli

Naples' best all-round bookshop with range of English-language literature.

Via San Tommaso d'Aquino 70/76 081 764 2111; www.lafeltrinelli.it
R2, R3

Fratelli Tramontano

Renowned for its *haute couture* leather goods.

✉ Via Chiaia 143 ☎ 081 414 837 🚌 R2, R3

Gambardella

A treasure trove of everything to do with paper – wrapping paper, gift bags, boxes, cards, ribbons and stationery in over 500 designs, many made on site.

✉ Largo Corpo di Napoli 3 ☎ 081 552 1333 🚌 E1

Marinella

Made-to-measure ties for celebrities, heads of state and VIPs.

✉ Riviera di Chiaia 287 ☎ 081 245 1182 🚌 R2, R3

La Rinascente

Quality clothes, perfumes and household goods.

✉ Via Toledo 340 ☎ 081 411 511

Scaturchio

Historic pastry shop famous for its *sfogliatelle* and house specialities; *zeffiro all'arancia* (orange delicacy), and chocolate and rum *ministeriale* (► 61).

✉ Piazza San Domenico Maggiore 19 ☎ 081 551 6944

ENTERTAINMENT

CLASSICAL MUSIC

Auditorium RAI-TV

The national TV network's concert hall stages both classical music and jazz.

✉ Via Guglielmo Marconi (Fuorigrotta) ☎ 081 725 1506/1111 (RAI switchboard)

Bellini

Only recently resumed, with both drama and operatic productions.

✉ Via Conte di Ruvo 17 ☎ 081 549 9688; www.teatrobellini.it 🚌 R1, R4

Conservatorio San Pietro a Majella

Housed since 1826 in a handsome 14th-century convent, the Music Conservatory has two concert halls, the Alessandro Scarlatti for orchestral concerts and the smaller Giuseppe Martucci for chamber music recitals.

✉ Via San Pietro a Majella 35 ☎ www.sanpeitroamajella.it 🚌 R1, R4

Teatro delle Palme

Chamber music recitals are staged here by the Associazione Scarlatti.

✉ Via Vetriera 12 ☎ 081 418 134; www.associazionescarlatti.it 🚌 R3

Teatro San Carlo

One of the world's most beautiful opera houses (➤ 104–105), the theatre stages opera, ballet and symphonic concerts played by its resident Orchestra Sinfonica and guest orchestras. The season runs from November to June.

✉ Via San Carlo 98/F ☎ 081 797 2330/2412/2314; www.teatrosancarlo.it 🚌 C25, R2, R3

CLUBS

The city's club scene changes fast. Chiaia's Piazza dei Martiri is a mob scene, Piazza Bellini lively but more sedate. *Qui Napoli* publishes up-to-date listings, but here are a few 'institutions'.

Around Midnight

A friendly and long-established jazz club and bar.

✉ Via Giuseppe Bonito 32 ☎ 081 558 2834; www.aroundmidnight.it

Madison Street

Naples' biggest disco caters to a trendy crowd attracted by the different theme nights – gay on Saturday.

✉ Via Sgambati 47 ☎ 081 546 4930

La Mela

More elegant than most in the fashionable Chiaia district.

✉ Via dei Mille 40 ☎ 081 410 270

Bay of Naples

The beauty of the Bay of Naples is almost too perfect – the bold curve around the city itself, the romantic profile of Mount Vesuvius, and beyond, the rugged Sorrento peninsula, all flanked by the sentinel islands of Capri and Ischia.

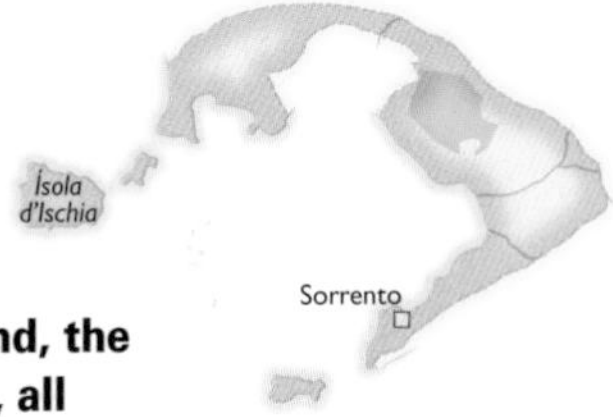

Despite the vaporous fumaroles of the Campi Flegrei to the west and the urban monstrosities around the ancient ruins of Pompei and Herculaneum to the east, beauty prevails. Away from the metropolitan sprawl, the clear coastal waters are suffused with the bay's unique luminosity to produce truly emerald green and sapphire blue grottoes. And the splendours of Roman antiquity survive, from the Pompeian houses and shops to the imperial villas of Capri.

CAPRI

The colours and fragrance of Capri's Mediterranean and subtropical vegetation, elegant patrician villas, romantic Roman ruins amid mountain greenery, overlooking blue waters washing over secluded coves and mysterious grottoes – all seduce the willing visitor. Emperor Tiberius was charmed into building 12 villas here, and countless painters and poets have forgotten to go home.

Hydrofoils and ferries serve Capri from Naples, Sorrento and Positano. Take a fast hydrofoil (35 minutes from Naples, 20 from Sorrento), or a slower, cheaper ferry. All-in day excursions are expensive, so visit Capri on your own. From the port of Marina Grande local buses run to Capri town and Anacapri, or take the harbourside funicular which will whisk you up to the town. Round-island tours and trips to the Grotta Azzurra also leave from here.

www.capritourism.com

27r Marina Grande-Capri; Marina Grande-Anacapri; Capri-Anacapri; Anacapri-Grotta Azzurra Caremar (Naples, Sorrento, Positano) 081 837 0700; www.caremar.it Capri permits personally owned cars year round, hire cars from 1 Nov to 1 Apr. Best form of transport is the local bus or boat

Anacapri

Anacapri – 'high Capri' – lies to the west of the island, with Monte Solaro looming above. Isolated for centuries, its inhabitants are farmers, known for their independent attitudes. The hub of this scattered community is Piazza Vittoria, from where a **chairlift** whisks you up to the top of Monte Solaro. Across the road, Via San Nicola leads to the church of San Michele Arcangelo.

Via Giuseppe Orlandi 59 081 837 1524

Chairlift

Mar–Oct 9:30 to one hour before sunset; Nov–Apr 10:30–3. Closed Tue in winter 081 837 1428 Moderate

Capri town

Impossibly picturesque, glitzy and glamorous, Capri town is the island's main settlement, a maze of flower-hung alleys, exquisite villas and stylish shops and restaurants. Its hub is the Piazzetta (officially Piazza Umberto I), from where narrow streets lead outwards. Take Via Vittorio Emanuele, which leads, via Via Matteoti, to the Giardini di Augusto (open dawn–dusk), a terraced garden with fabulous views over the harbour of Marina Piccola and the three rock stacks known as the Faraglioni. You can walk down the twisting Via Krupp to the sea, or head to the **Certosa di San Giacomo,** once Capri's most important monastery.

Piazza Umberto 1 081 837 0686

Certosa di San Giacomo

Viale Certosa 40 081 837 6218 Tue–Sat 9–2, Sun 9–1

Inexpensive Buses to Marina Grande, Marina Piccola and Anacapri

Grotta Azzurra

Best places to see, ➤ 38–39.

Villa Jovis

Best preserved of Emperor Tiberius's villas on Capri, the ruins of this grand residence sprawl across the island's eastern

promontory. Built around three vast cisterns for storing rainwater, the imperial apartments are on the north side, bathhouses to the south, and servants' quarters to the west. The view across the bay to Vesuvius was the emperor's parting gift to enemies hurled over the precipice known as Salto di Tiberio (Tiberius Jump).

www.villajovis.it

✉ Viale Amadeo Maturi ☎ 081 837 4549 ⌚ Daily 9 to one hour before sunset. Closed 1 Jan , Easter Sun, 2 Jun, 15 Aug, 25 Dec ✋ Inexpensive

Villa San Michele

A short walk from Anacapri's Piazza Vittoria, this villa and its lovely garden are a charming monument to Axel Munthe (1857–1949), Swedish author of *The Story of San Michele*. Built by the writer-physician himself, the house is an eclectic mix of styles, combining baroque furnishings and Roman antiquities.

✉ Viale Axel Munthe 3 ☎ 081 837 1401 ⌚ May–Sep 9–6; Apr and Oct 9:30–5; Mar 9:30–4:30; Nov–Feb 10:30–3:30 ✋ Moderate

More to see in the Bay of Naples

CAMPI FLEGREI AND THE SPA TOWNS

Volcanic activity in the Phlegrean (Greek for 'burning') Fields fascinated ancient Romans and later European aristocrats on the Grand Tour. They came hoping for a (mild) eruption and to bathe in the hot springs. Today, much of the area is covered with ugly modern buildings, though conservationists are fighting back, and a large tract now forms part of the Parco dei Campi Flegrei, created in 2008 to preserve both the archaeological riches and the remaining unspoilt natural parts of the area. The Astroni woodlands, once used by King Alfonso of Aragon for hunting, are now a nature reserve. Pozzuoli, originally a Greek trading port (in the 6th century BC), is the region's largest town and has a large **Roman amphitheatre.** In the slumbering **Solfatara** crater on the eastern outskirts, with mudpools and sulphurous fumaroles.

Baia and Bacoli remain the fashionable seaside resorts they were for ancient Romans. One attraction is the ruin of an imperial villa in Baia's **Parco Archeologico.** Cuma, one of the western Mediterranean's oldest Greek colonies (750BC), has romantic ruins overgrown with vines, two Greek temples, a Roman forum and the Antro della Sibilla (Cave of the Cumaean Sybil), from which the prophetess dispensed her wisdom.

27p Pozzuoli, Bacoli, Baia (€–€€) Ferrovia Cumana from Montesanto (Naples) Via Campi Flegrei, 3 Pozzuoli 081 526 1481/9198

Anfiteatro Flavio (Roman amphitheatre)

Via Terracciano 75, Pozzuoli 081 526 6007 Wed–Mon 9 to 1 hour before sunset, closed Tue Moderate

Solfatara

Via Solfatara 161, Pozzuoli 081 526 2341 Daily 8:30 to 1 hour before sunset Inexpensive

Parco Archeologico di Baia

Via Fusaro 37 081 868 7592 Tue–Sun 9 to 1 hour before sunset Inexpensive

HERCULANEUM

In an enclosure within the modern town of Ercolano, Herculaneum is less immediately spectacular than Pompei (➤ 126–129), but more compact and generally better preserved. Even a short visit gives a clear idea of what an ancient Roman town looked like. Whereas the eruption of AD79 destroyed Pompei with volcanic cinders, it buried Herculaneum under rivers of hot mud, creating a protective crust up to 20m (65ft) thick. Houses survived with one and even two upper storeys and woodwork intact, though they were stripped of paintings by Bourbon excavators in the 18th century. The excavated part – much, perhaps most, of the site is still buried under the modern town – suggests a leisured aristocratic community compared to more commercially oriented Pompei.

The town's grid plan runs south from its main street, Decumanus Maximus, to a promontory once much closer to the sea. The bay view made this a choice neighbourhood. The large Casa dei Cervi, House of the Stags (Cardus V), is named after its sculpture of stags being attacked by dogs. It also depicts a very drunk Hercules. On Cardus IV are impressive multiple family dwellings with two upper floors: Casa del Tramezzo di Legno (House of the Wooden Partition) and Casa Graticcio (Lattice House), with a balcony overlooking the street. Further north, Casa del Mobilo Carbonizzato (House of the Charred Furniture) retains a divan bed and a small table. Next door, the wine merchant's Casa di Nettuno (House of Neptune) has a miraculously preserved ground-floor counter, utensils, shelves of wine jars and, in its courtyard, a pretty green and blue mosaic of Neptune and his wife, Amphitrite.

28q Scavi (excavations), Corso Resina 081 857 5347 Daily Apr–Oct 8:30–7:30 (last ticket 6); Nov–Mar 8:30–5 (last ticket 3:30). Closed 1 Jan, May, 25 Dec Expensive Cafés (€) near tourist office
Circumvesuviana (from Naples or Sorrento) to Ercolano 254, 255
Guided tours available
Via IV Novembre 82 081 788 1243

ISCHIA

As Pithecusa (Monkey Island), Ischia was the Greek settlers' first Italian foothold (800BC) before they went on to colonize Cuma 50 years later (► 119). Geologically, the island is a volcanic extension of the Campi Flegrei (► 119) via the two stepping-stone isles of Procida and tiny Vivara, a nature reserve. The only volcanic activity apparent today is the hot springs, notable at the fashionable resorts of Casamicciola Terme and Lacco Ameno.

Lacco Ameno's modest little Museo Archeologico displays finds from the ancient Greek settlement, including 'Nestor's Cup' with the oldest known inscription of Greek verse, dating from the time that Homer's epics were first written down.

The main harbour town of Ischia Porto is a largely 18th-century development, with Terme Comunali (public spa facilities) just beyond the port. Porto stretches through Ischia Ponte to the Castello Aragonese, an ancient fortress dating from the 5th century BC, with splendid views.

Fast-growing Forio is the most popular west coast resort, with its landmark silhouette of the gleaming white 16th-century Santuario del Soccorso. Just outside town, British composer Sir William Walton built his villa, **La Mortella,** which is famous for its garden planted with magnolia and palm trees.

26q From major towns, island circuit 2.5 hours, CD buses clockwise, CS counter-clockwise Hydrofoil from Naples (Molo Beverello) to Ischia Port or Forio, Alilauro 081 761 1004 Via Antonio Sogliuzzo 72 081 507 4211

La Mortella

Via F Calise 35, Forio 081 986 220; www.lamortella.it
Apr to mid-Nov Tue, Thu, Sat, Sun 9–7 Expensive

a drive around the Sorrento Peninsula

This tour takes in the peninsula's rugged north coast, the plains of citrus groves and mountains of the interior, with spectacular views over both the Bay of Naples (➤ 115–136) and the west end of the Amalfi Coast (➤ 137–152).

On the A3 autostrada from Naples, fork south to the Castellammare di Stabia exit to start the drive. From Castellammare's Villa Quisisana, S145 hairpins up Monte Faito before heading back down to the coast to Vico Equense.

Castellammare di Stabia (ancient Stabiae) has been a renowned spa resort since Roman antiquity. It was buried by the Vesuvius eruption of AD79, but was quickly rebuilt. It has a medieval castle and the Antiquarium Stabiae exhibiting archaeological finds. On Monte Faito, woods of ash, chestnut and pine alternate with meadows, vineyards and olive groves. Earthquake and war destroyed all Vico Equense's historic treasures, apart from a Gothic church and medieval gate.

From Vico, the road continues to Meta where it forks west to Sant'Agnello and Sorrento (➤ 130). At the west end of the ever-popular resort, S145 turns left up to Sant'Agata.

For those not lunching in Sorrento, Sant'Agata sui due Golfi is home to one of Italy's most prestigious – and expensive – gourmet restaurants (Don Alfonso, ➤ 135–136) plus, absolutely free, a magnificent view over both the Bay of Naples and the Bay of Salerno.

From Sant'Agata an optional detour down to the peninsula's south coast at Marina di Cantone will add a 45-minute drive each way before continuing to the end of the drive at Positano (➤ 46–47).

Marina di Cantone is a little beach resort much appreciated by the sailing fraternity for its seafood restaurants. The road east to Positano offers a first glimpse of the charms of the Amalfi Coast.

Distance 85–110km (53–68 miles), depending on detours
Time Allow a day
Start point Castellamare di Stabia ✚ *29q*
End point Positano ✚ *29r*
Lunch O'Parrucchiano (€–€€) ✉ Corso Italia 71, Sorrento
☎ 081 878 1321

POMPEI

This is the stuff of ancient Roman daily life. We are its privileged witnesses today, thanks to the town's tragic burial under volcanic ash in AD79 and its miraculous preservation until excavations began in 1748. Along with its temples, town hall, theatres and other public buildings, the shops and houses are still here, the market, the bakery and brothel, the wine shop and grocery store – and poignant remains of people trapped in the catastrophe. Once located much closer to the sea than it is today, at the mouth of the Sarno River, Pompei prospered as a distribution centre for farming produce – wheat, olives, table grapes and wine – from the surrounding communities. Its population was perhaps 20,000 to 30,000.

The visit divides conveniently into public buildings and private houses. Original frescoes and sculptures are still in place, but some are exhibited in Naples' Museo Archeologico Nazionale (➤ 42–43).

The Forum is up the road from the Porta Marina entrance. Left and right of the entrance to the main square is a temple to Apollo and a basilica housing the chamber of commerce and courthouse. The Forum was flanked on three sides by two-storey porticoes of Doric and Ionic columns. At the south end, in front of the municipal offices, are plinths for statues of politicians, and a white platform for orators. At the far end is the six-columned Capitolium (shrine) dedicated to Jupiter, Juno and Minerva. In the northeast corner, the porticoed Macellum was the town's main food market.

Via della Abbondanza was a busy thoroughfare leading east from the south end of the Forum; the curved stone paving is rutted by chariot wheels and has raised pedestrian crossings. The walls are scratched or daubed in red with ancient graffiti – insults, obscene drawings, advertising and election campaign slogans. To the left, on Vico Lupanare (Brothel Alley) is one of Pompei's 25 registered brothels, a two-storey building with naughty frescoes.

The Terme Stabiane (Stabian Baths), back on Via della Abbondanza, are built around a porticoed *palaestra* (gymnasium) with a swimming pool to the left. On the right, beyond the vestibule, men undressed in the *apodyterium* and went from *tepidarium* (warm) to *caldarium* (hot) rooms before cooling off in the *frigidarium*. The women's baths are beyond the furnaces north of the *caldarium*.

The Teatro Grande seated 5,000 spectators to watch the plays of Plautus and Terence, and also gladiators whose *caserma* (barracks) were behind the stage in the large *quadriporticus* (rectangular building). The smaller, originally roofed, Teatro Piccolo probably staged concerts and poetry recitals.

Of the surviving private houses, three north of the Forum stand out. Casa dei Vetii, belonging to two wealthy ex-slaves, is built around two sides of a columned, peristyle garden. A bold priapic figure in the entrance hall is just the first of many superb wall-paintings. The palatial Casa del Fauno is named after the bronze faun statue in its courtyard, brought to Pompei from Alexandria in the 2nd century BC. It has fine mosaics, a majestic colonnade and a formal garden planted with shrubs common in antiquity. Casa del Poeta Tragico is famous for its threshold mosaic, a fierce chained dog and the timeless inscription *Cave Canem* (Beware of the Dog).

www.pompeiisites.org
29q Pompei Scavi, Porta Marina
081 857 5347 Daily Apr–Oct 8:30–7:30 (last ticket 6); Nov–Mar 8:30–5 (last ticket 3:30). Closed 1 Jan, May, 25 Dec Expensive: ticket includes main site and Villa dei Misteri (➤ 52–53)
Pleasant cafeteria (€) near the Forum
Circumvesuviana: Pompei–Scavi (Villa dei Misteri) English-language tours with official guides; maps for self-guided tours from ticket office
Via Sacra 1 081 850 8451 or 081 850 7255

SORRENTO

The clifftop resort, which enjoyed a heyday in the 19th century, remains popular as a base from which to explore the Sorrento peninsula and beyond. Sitting on a natural terrace with a sheer drop to the sea and ravines on either side, the town is surrounded by lovely gardens. Its name is linked by legend to the sirens who tried to lure Ulysses and his sailors on to the rocks below.

Piazza Tasso is the gateway to Sorrento's *centro storico* (historic centre). A major monument here is the art nouveau Grand Hotel Vittoria, with ancient marble columns in its gardens left from its predecessor, the villa of Emperor Augustus. Medieval Via Pietà leads to the heart of the old town past the 13th-century Byzantine-style Palazzo Veniero (No 14) and 15th-century Palazzo Correale (No 24), now part of the baroque Santa Maria della Pietà.

Across from the campanile of the cathedral, Via Giuliani leads to the Sedile Dominova. This 15th-century arcaded loggia, where the town's nobles held their council, is today a club for card-players.

The **Museo Correale di Terranova** houses a family collection of Greek and Roman antiquities, Neapolitan painting and European porcelain, glass and clocks, and old prints of Sorrento.

www.sorrentotourism.com

28r Naples Capodichino airport bus; SITA for Amalfi Coast Circumvesuviana from Naples (Corso Garibaldi) Hydrofoil from Naples Alilauro 081 497 2238 hydrofoil to Capri and Amalfi Coast 081 807 1812 Via Luigi De Maio 35 081 807 4033/877 3397

Museo Correale di Terranova

Via Correale 48 081 878 1846 Daily 9–2. Closed Tue and public hols Expensive

VESUVIUS (MONTE VESUVIO)

Best places to see, ➤ 40–41.

VILLA DEI MISTERI

Best places to see, ➤ 52–53.

a walk around Sorrento

This is a pleasant walk round the pretty resort of Sorrento, taking in the *centro storico* (historic centre), some medieval cloisters and the best shopping areas.

Start in Piazza Tasso facing the sea, and look down into the ravine that gives access to Marina Piccola, home to the ferry port and the town's beaches and bathing establishments. Turn left past the ceramic shop and follow the road that curves down to Piazza Sant'Antonino

This is home to the Basilica di Sant'Antonino, named after Sorrento's patron saint, whose tomb lies in the 18th-century crypt. From here, Via San Francesco swings left to the church of San Francesco, beside which you'll find the entrance to the 14th-century cloister, where ogival arches surround a pretty garden.

Exiting the cloister, cross the road diagonally to the entrance of the Villa Comunale. Stroll through for fabulous views across the bay, and a peek at the steps leading down the cliffs to the lidos below. Leave the park, and head up Via Giuliani for two blocks, crossing Via Accademia.

At the next junction, you'll find yourself on Via Cesareo, a narrow street in the heart of the old town, home to a plethora of gift shops of every description, where you can buy everything from local ceramics, soaps and scents to locally produced *limoncello.*

Follow Via Cesareo, then turn left up Via Tasso to Corso Italia, Sorrento's smartest shopping street, and the Duomo (cathedral).

It was rebuilt in the 15th century and inside are some 16th- and 17th-century paintings and some beautiful intarsia, inlaid wood work, a Sorrentine speciality, in the choir stalls.

Walk past the Duomo up Via Sersale to the Piazza Antiche Mure, Turn right down Via degli Aranci which leads down to the far end of the Corso Italia. Turn right and head back along the street to reach Piazza Tasso.

Distance 2km (1,2 miles)
Time 1 hour easy walking
Start/end point Piazza Tasso
Lunch Il Fauno ✉ Piazza Tasso ☎ 081 878 7735. Sorrento's smartest bar is one of the best people-watching spots in town

HOTELS

CAPRI

Quisisana (€€€)

Originally a high-class 19th-century sanatorium, now one of the world's best-known luxury hotels. Facilities include tennis, gym, indoor and outdoor swimming pools and two restaurants.

✉ Via Camerelle 2 ☎ 081 837 0788; www.quisisana.com 🕔 Closed Nov–Mar

Villa Krupp (€€€)

Simple comfort in 12 rooms – originally home to Russian writer Maxim Gorky. Splendid view of Faraglioni rocks and Marina Piccola.

✉ Via Matteotti 12, near Parco Augusto; www.capritourism.com ☎ 081 837 0362 🕔 Closed Nov–Mar

ISCHIA

Il Monastero (€–€€)

An ancient monastery in the heart of the Castello has been tastefully converted into this peaceful and stylishly simple hotel, whose 22 rooms, housed in old monks' cells, have views over the sea. Lovely terrace for breakfast, relaxing, helpful staff and excellent value for money.

✉ Castello Aragonese ☎ 081 992 435; www.albergoilmonastero.it 🕔 Closed Nov–Easter

SORRENTO

Hotel Tourist (€–€€)

A family-run and friendly hotel that offers great value in the heart of town, with public transport near by. Rooms are spotless, all have air-conditioning and many have balconies, though front rooms can be noisy. There's an indoor bar and another beside the pool in the garden. Half-board rates are lower than those for room only.

✉ Corso Italia 315 ☎ 081 878 2086; www.hoteltourist.it

RESTAURANTS

BAIA

L'Altro Cucchiaro (€€€)

One of Italy's finest seafood restaurants overlooking Baia's pretty harbour. Follow fresh *fritturine* (fried whitebait) with *gnocchi* or *spaghettini* in seafood sauce, or oven-baked *rana pescatrice* (monkfish). Terrific desserts.

✉ Via Lucullo 13, Baia Porto ☎ 081 868 7196 🕐 Dinner only. Closed Sun, Mon, Aug

CAPRI

Da Gemma (€€)

This restaurant is set beneath the arches of the old town, with lovely views outside. The food is traditional and reliable – expect good pasta and pizza, baked fish and fresh salads.

✉ Via Madre Serafina 6 ☎ 081 837 0461 🕐 Closed Nov–Mar

Gran Caffè

See page 60.

La Savardina da Edoardo

See page 61.

Villa Brunella

See page 61.

ISCHIA

Alberto Ischia (€€€)

Come to this lovely restaurant, with tables set on a platform above the sea, to enjoy a memorable dinner of typical island dishes that might include a marinated *carpaccio* of local fish and pasta with a sea bass, baby tomato and almond sauce. Booking advised

✉ Via Cristoforo Colombo 8 ☎ 081 981 259 🕐 Closed Nov to mid-Mar

SANT'AGATA

Don Alfonso (€€€)

One of southern Italy's most celebrated restaurants is in this pretty

pink villa. House specialities include *cipolla novella farcita* (spring onions stuffed with shrimp and bacon), *penne alle calamarette* (pasta with baby squid) andd *capretto lucano* (goat kid).
✉ Piazza Sant'Agata ☎ 081 878 0026 ⊕ Closed Mon; Tue in winter and a period during Feb–Mar

SORRENTO

O Parrucchiano

See page 60.

Sant'Anna da Emilia (€€)

This friendly little restaurant right beside the sea at Sorrento's old fishing harbour serves traditional local pasta dishes and freshly caught fish and seafood.
✉ Via Marina Grande 62 ☎ 081 807 2720 ⊕ Closed Tue, Nov–Mar lunch only

SHOPPING

Canfora

Famous since 1946 for handmade, classic shoes.
✉ Via Camerelle 3, Capri ☎ 081 837 0487; www.canfora.com

Limonoro

You can sample before you buy at this manufacturer of *limoncello*, the classic lemon liqueur of the region. The factory is part of the shop and there are bottles of every shape and size for sale.
✉ Via San Cesareo 49/53, Sorrento ☎ 081 807 2782

Mennella

Traditional island craftwork, pottery and majolica tiling.
✉ Casamicciola Terme, Via Salvatore Girardi 47, Ischia ☎ 081 994 442

Siniscalchi

Beautiful summer sandals, made on the premises in fine leather in every style and colour. If you can't find something to suit, they'll custom make it for you in a couple of days.
✉ Via San Cesareo 83, Sorrento ☎ 081 877 1515

The Amalfi Coast

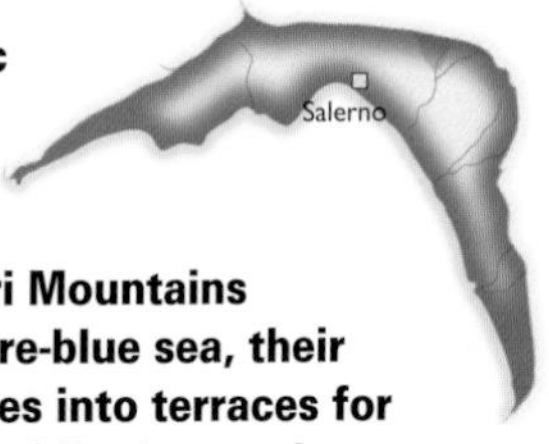

One of the world's most idyllic stretches of coast, the Costiera Amalfitana, runs along the south side of the Sorrento peninsula. The Lattari Mountains plunge precipitously to an azure-blue sea, their slopes carved over the centuries into terraces for vines, citrus and olive groves, while tiny settlements and elegant villas, linked by ancient pathways rich in wild flowers, perch high above the water.

The famous S163 highway winds sinuously along the coast towards Amalfi, built along a narrow valley. En route, Positano's jumble of colour-washed houses hug the steep cliffs above a tiny beach and harbour, while inland, Ravello stands high above the sea, its views the essence of Mediterranean beauty. Lookout towers and fortresses punctuate the coast, a reminder of the historic strategic importance of what today is one of Italy's most beguiling holiday playgrounds.

AMALFI

The town's cosmopolitan atmosphere is not something new; Amalfi's central position on the Bay of Salerno marked it out early for a maritime destiny. Starting as a Byzantine protectorate in AD839, it developed – along with Venice and well before Pisa and Genoa – a commercial empire throughout the Mediterranean.

From the Arabs Amalfi acquired not only architectural models for its duomo (cathedral) and Chiostro del Paradiso (Cloister of Paradise; ➤ 37), but also the nautical compass to gain a navigational headstart on its rivals. In its 10th- and 11th-century heyday it had trading posts from Tunis to Alexandria and Antioch, and was halted only by the Normans.

From Piazza Duomo, explore the medieval arcades of Via dei Mercanti (or Ruga Nova) from the foot of the cathedral campanile to the Porta dell'Ospedale. The whitewashed passageway opens

out onto little gardens, the Church of Santa Maria Addolorata and the Capo de Ciuccio fountain. On the way are charming antique shops, wine merchants and shops specializing in the locally distilled *limoncello* (lemon liqueur), and potent fruity variations. A popular excursion, just 4km (2.5 miles) west of town, is to the **Grotta di Smeralda,** a cave where the waters are as brilliantly emerald green as those of Capri's Grotta Azzurra are sapphire blue.

29r Excellent cafés, pizzerias and restaurants around Piazza del Duomo (€–€€€) SITA (from Naples, Sorrento and all coastal resorts) Metro del Mare 199 600 700 To beat the high season traffic, take the hydrofoil or ferry between Positano, Amalfi and Salerno Via delle Repubbliche Marinare 27 089 871 107; www.amalfitouristoffice.com

Grotta di Smeralda

Statale 163, Conca dei Marini Daily 9–4 Moderate

DUOMO DI AMALFI

Best places to see, ➤ 36–37.

PAESTUM

The ancient Greek city of Paestum, founded in the 6th century BC and absorbed into the Roman empire in the 2nd century AD, is chiefly renowned for its three Greek temples and extensive Roman ruins. Rising majestically from fields by the sea, their honey-coloured stone columns bear witness to Greek colonial prosperity in southern Italy, in particular Poseidonia, as it was known before the Roman conquest in 273BC. This is perhaps appropriate for a colony founded by traders from Sybaris, whose taste for high living gave rise to the word 'sybarite'.

To explore the site, pass through the ancient walls to explore the Temple of Ceres (500BC), a Greek Doric masterpiece standing at the head of a Roman road leading south to the amphitheatre and Roman forum, built over much of the Greek city.

South from here is the superb Temple of Neptune (➤ 50–51), built of local limestone that was once faced with marble. The same technique was used on the 6th-century BC Temple of Hera, rising dreamlike from the plain to the south.

Don't miss the **Museo Archeologico** which exhibits Paestum's sculpture, ceramics and other works of art, most notably the Tomba del Tuffatore (Diver's Tomb) from the 5th century BC, a rare example of Greek mural painting.

www.infopaestum.it

32s Via Magna Grecia Daily 9am to one hour before sunset

Moderate (expensive if combining site and museum) Nettuno (€–€€), Via Principe di Piemonte 2. Lunch only. Closed Mon in winter 082 881 1028

From Salerno, Piazza Concordia

Paestum on Salerno–Reggio di Calabria line Guided tours; occasional lectures. Concerts and plays in summer 0828 811 016

Via Magna Grecia 87 082 722 322

Museo Archeologico

82 881 1023 Daily 9–7. Closed first and third Mon in the month

POSITANO

Best places to see, ➤ 46–47.

a drive from Positano to Salerno

This is the famous Amalfi Drive along the coast road, taking in the 'Big Three' resorts: Positano (➤ 46–47), Amalfi (➤ 138–139) and Ravello (➤ 144–145). But on the way, it also offers a glimpse of smaller fishing villages and market towns such as Praiano, Atrani and Vietri, and briefly leaves the coastal highway after Amalfi for an incursion inland to look at the Lattari Mountains. It is particularly worthwhile going on to Salerno (➤ 146) if you are planning an excursion down to Paestum (➤ 140–141).

From Positano, turn east and stay on the S163 until just after Amalfi, at Atrani. On this road more than most, keep well to the right and do not hesitate to use the horn on blind curves.

Praiano's fishermen's houses are scattered across the ridge of Monte Sant'Angelo, and Marina di Praia is a charming little beach. Just before Conca dei Marini are signposts for the translucent green waters of the Grotta di Smeralda (➤ 139). Atrani is one of the coast's prettiest little towns, particularly on Piazza Umberto I.

About 1km (0.5 miles) after Atrani, turn left at the Ravello exit. From the tunnel passing under Ravello, go left on the highway signposted Valico Chiunzi. Continue to the crossroads on the crest of the Lattari Mountain ridge, then turn right to take the highway back to the coast, signposted Maiori.

This detour loops around the Tramonti plain, with some impressive rugged mountain views along the way. At this altitude, orange and lemon trees are replaced with vineyards and vegetable gardens with aubergines (eggplants), tomatoes and bell-peppers.

At Maiori, turn left on to the S163 to continue via Vietri to Salerno.

Vietri is famous for its majolica ceramics, both for domestic and monumental use. Notice the dome on the parish church of San Giovanni Battista.

Distance 70–80km (40–50 miles)
Time Take a whole day
Start point Positano ✚ *29r* **End point** Salerno ✚ *30q*
Lunch Le Arcate (€–€€) ✉ Via G Di Benedetto 4, Atrani
☎ 089 871 367

RAVELLO

Some 350m (1,150ft) above the coast, perched on a ridge flanked by the valleys of the Dragone and Reginna, Ravello is a place apart, an idyllic, flower-hung town of sumptuous villas, historic buildings and verdant gardens. Ancient Romans fled here from invading Visigoths and Huns; today, holidaymakers come to escape the crowds on the coast. Strolling around the gardens and looking out to sea, it is easy to forget the outside world.

The medieval connection with the Duchy of Amalfi, and the lucrative role Ravello played in trade with Sicily, becomes clear both in the town's churches and its older villas, each showing the influence of Byzantine and Arab architectural styles – most notably the lovely Villa Rufolo (➤ 54–55), opposite the Duomo. The 11th-century cathedral has been restored to its original appearance, while its 13th-century campanile, with its handsome twin-mullioned windows, has the characteristic intertwining arches of Arab architecture. Inside the church, the two richly decorated marble pulpits, borne aloft by six lions, capture the opulent style of the eastern Mediterranean. North of the Duomo, these elements reappear in the multiple-domed 12th-century Church of San Giovanni del Toro.

At the southern end of Ravello, the grandiose **Villa Cimbrone** was built in the 18th century and ingeniously incorporates ancient columns and medieval sculpture from the town's various churches and *palazzi*. Its splendid garden with a belvedere at the far edge of the Ravello ridge was landscaped by Lord Grimthorpe, designer of the clock mechanism for London's Big Ben.

29q Cafés, restaurants (€–€€) around Piazza Duomo SITA bus many times daily from Naples, hourly from Amalfi 6am–9pm Summer musical festival (➤ 25)

Villa Cimbrone

Via Santa Chiara 26 089 857 459; www.villacimbrone.com

May–Sep 9–6; Oct–Apr 9am to sunset Moderate

Via Roma 18/bis 089 857 096; www.ravellotime.it

SALERNO

Scene of the Allied landings in 1943, Salerno, a key industrial port, has a long history. War – and earthquake – have destroyed much of what was once an important university town, famous for its medical school since the Middle Ages, and today, little of the medieval city remains. What is left comprises a few narrow lanes around Via Portacatena and chic Via dei Mercanti, but Salerno's chief treasure is its magnificent Duomo (cathedral), built in 1076 by the town's Norman conqueror, Robert Guiscard.

The alterations carried out in the 17th and 18th centuries incorporated the existing architectural elements – Greek, Byzantine and Romanesque. Pick of these is the main entrance, the Porta dei Leoni, adorned with Romanesque sculpted lions, Arab arches and Greek columns. Inside, don't miss the lavish baroque crypt, built to house the supposed relics of St Matthew the Apostle. Over the double altar are two bronze statues of the saint (1622). The museum next door contains an early medieval altar-font, embellished with 54 superb ivory panels. From here, head uphill to take in the Castello di Arechi, part of the old defence system, which has spectacular views over the town and sea.

30q SITA from Naples and Amalfi Coast resorts Ferries from Positano, Amalfi (Metro del Mare 199 600 700; www.metrodelmare.com)
Piazza Vittorio Veneto 1 089 231 432; www.salernocity.com

VILLA RUFOLO, RAVELLO

Best places to see, ➤ 54–55.

HOTELS

AMALFI

La Bussola (€–€€)

Pleasant family hotel nicely situated on harbour promenade.

✉ Via Lungomare dei Cavalieri 16 ☎ 089 871 533; www.labussolahotel.it

Hotel Amalfi (€€)

Just up from the main square, this hotel is good value, with large, bright rooms – many large enough to sleep 3 or 4. Some have balconies, and there's a roof terrace and pretty garden shaded by citrus trees. Rates drop in winter.

✉ Vico dei Pastai 3 ☎ 089 872 440; www.hamalfi.it

Villa Lara (€€)

Intimate, six-room three-star hotel in garden setting with fine views.

✉ Via delle Cartiere 1 ☎ 089 873 6358; www.villalara.it

PAESTUM

Villa Rita (€)

Stay here and you can stroll down the road to admire the temples by moonlight. Set in a pretty garden right in the archaeological zone, the hotel has a good-sized pool, airy rooms, a welcoming lounge and bar, an excellent restaurant and a peaceful atmosphere.

✉ Via Principe di Piemonte 5, Zona Archeologica ☎ 0828 723 634; www.hotelvillarita.it 🕒 Closed Nov to mid-Mar

POSITANO

La Fenice (€€)

This complex of rooms spreads on either side of the main coast road, with seven rooms in the main villa and eight in a little villette below. From here, a path runs down to the tiny beach and sea-water pool. Furnishings are bright and functional, some rooms have private terraces, and the owners are very welcoming. A delicious breakfast is served on the shady terraces. No credit cards accepted.

✉ Via Marconi 4 ☎ 089 875 513

Sirenuse (€€€)
One of southern Italy's finest hotels. Rooms are furnished with exquisite taste in traditional Mediterranean style. First-class restaurant and the coast's prettiest swimming pool.
✉ Via Cristoforo Colombo 30 ☎ 089 875 066; www.sirenuse.it

RAVELLO

Palumbo (€€€)
Opulent hotel occupying medieval Palazzo Confalone, which Wagner made his home while working on *Parsifal*. The spacious rooms have lovely garden views.
✉ Via San Giovanni del Toro 16 ☎ 089 857 244; www.hotelpalumbo.it

Villa Cimbrone (€€€)
Housed in the main building of the famous garden, this opulent hotel combines elegance, romance and charm to provide the perfect hideaway. Expect frescoes, antique tiles, period furniture with mod cans added. The beautiful pool and private area of the gardens overlook the sea, as do many of the bedroom balconies.
✉ Via Santa Chiara 26 ☎ 089 857 459; www.villacimbrone.com

RESTAURANTS

AMALFI

La Caravella (€€€)
Amalfi's finest restaurant doubles as an *enoteca* (wine shop) and ceramic gallery, but it's the food that draws in the crowds. Try pasta dishes with saffron and prawns or squid stuffed with courgettes before moving on to the best of the day's catch, wrapped in lemon leaves and simply grilled.
✉ Via Matteo Camera 12 ☎ 089 871 029 🕐 Closed Tue, mid-Nov to Dec

Da Gemma (€€€)
Over 120 years old and still going strong. Try the wonderfully rich fish soup, the *linguine all'aragosta* (spiny lobster), or fresh fish, grilled or in white wine sauce. There's also a fine wine cellar.
✉ Via Lorenzo d'Amalfi and Fra'Gerardo Sasso 10, near Piazza del Duomo
☎ 089 871 1345 🕐 Closed Wed in winter, and 15 Jan–15 Feb

Da Maria (€€)

A delightful, friendly trattoria serving regional dishes, good fresh vegetables, varied *antipasti*, seafood pasta, the best of the local wines and great pizza.

✉ Via Lorenzo d'Amalfi 14, just off Piazza del Duomo ☎ 089 871 880 ⏲ Closed Mon

PAESTUM

Nonna Scepa (€€)

The archaeological site is surrounded by a plethora of restaurants catering for tourists, but head here for something a cut above the rest – home-made pasta, great fish and seafood and a wide selection of excellent pizzas.

✉ Via Laura, 45, Capaccio-Paestum ☎ 082 885 1064 ⏲ Closed Thu Oct–May

POSITANO

La Buca di Bacco (€€–€€€)

Beachfront trattoria popular with families and yachters for snacks and sumptuous gourmet cuisine, fresh seafood and pastas.

✉ Via Rampa Teglia 4 ☎ 089 875 699 ⏲ Closed Nov–Mar

Il Capitano (€€€)

You'll need to book for an outside place at this highly rated terrace restaurant, whose tables overlook the sea from under a cool green pergola. The emphasis is on classic local cooking, using the finest ingredients in dishes such as seafood antipasti, pasta with anchovies and peppers and ravioli stuffed with lobster. There's a Neapolitan floor show every Sunday – better than it sounds.

✉ Via Pasitea 119 ☎ 089 875 011 ⏲ Closed Wed and Nov–Mar

RAVELLO

Cumpà Cosimo (€€)

Very popular with local residents as well as foreign celebrities for the unfailing quality of the pasta and seafood dishes, served in an agreeable atmosphere.

✉ Via Roma 44–46 ☎ 089 857 156 ⏲ Closed Mon Nov–Feb

Figli di Papà (€€)

Vaults and arches soar above the tables of this creative restaurant, in a 12th-century *palazzo*. The chef has put his own stamp on the traditional ingredients of both land and sea, producing food that's more imaginative and modern in style than other local places in this price range. Good wine list and attentive service.

Via della Marra 7–9 089 858 302 Closed Tue Oct–Mar and 2 weeks Nov, mid-Jan to mid-Feb

Palumbo (€€€)

Palatial dining in the medieval Palazzo Confalone, now a luxury hotel, with superb terrace view of the Amalfi Coast. Try *insalata di seppioline* (baby squid with walnuts and celery), ravioli with mint (*menta*) or *spigola all'arancia* (sea bass in orange sauce).

Via San Giovanni del Toro 16 089 857 244 Closed 6 Jan–15 Mar

SHOPPING

AMALFI

Amalfi nelle Stampe Antiche

Just across from the Duomo, this is a treasure trove of beautiful products in hand-stamped papers – note- and address books, folders, letter racks and boxes; they also carry a lovely range of old prints and reproductions showing Amalfi and the coast before the tourists arrived, which make unusual and attractive souvenirs.

Piazza Duomo 10 089 873 6374

Anna Mostacciuolo

This elegant store is filled with objets d'art, but the main draw is the jewellery, particularly the cameos and corals, a speciality of the Naples area. Classic pieces contrast with a chunkier, more contemporary style, in the wide range on offer.

Piazza Duomo 22 089 871 552

Milleunaceramica

This ceramic shop is something special, with all the pieces made locally and hand-painted with traditional designs – 18th-century patterns, sunflowers and lemons. There's everything from massive platters, lamps and jars to tiny bowls and dishes, perfect for slipping into a suitcase corner.

✉ Via Pietro Capuano 36 ☎ 089 872 670

POSITANO

Rachele

Ladies should come here to track down that Positano essential – a loose but beautifully cut dress, shift or sundress in finest linen or cotton that will carry you through with Italian style from dawn to dusk – vibrant colours, lovely detailing and they last for years.

✉ Via dei Mulini 15/B ☎ 089 875 962

Sapori e Profumi di Positano

Lemons are the theme in this pretty shop, where *limoncello* jostles with soap, body products, candles and lemon preserves of all sorts. The ceramics are beautiful, the food locally sourced – *the* place to buy something that will evoke the magic of this coast.

✉ Via dei Mulini 6 ☎ 089 812 055

ENTERTAINMENT

MUSIC, THEATRE AND DANCE

Paestum Festival

From July to September a series of performances and events are staged in the superb setting of the Greek temples at Paestum. Events range from classical Greek theatre, music and opera to modern dance and rock concerts – Bob Dylan headlined in 2008.

☎ 0828 811 016; www.infopaestum.it

Ravello Festival

This international music festival, originally inspired by Wagner's visit to the town, runs from July to October and offers a mixed programme of classical music concerts, recitals, cinema and dance. Events are staged all over town, the best by far being the gardens of the Villa Rufolo, where the orchestra performs on a platform backed by the incredible view down to the sea.

✉ Fondazione Ravello, Sala Frau, Viale Richard Wagner 5, Ravello

✉ 089 858 360; www.ravellofestival.com

NIGHTCLUBS

Africana

Off the coast road between Amalfi and Positano, Africana is far and away the best – and best known – of the coast's clubs. Housed above the sea in a grotto, it features a glass floor and some wild decor that are the backdrop to the area's most serious clubbing.

✉ Off coast road at km 22–23 ✉ 089 874 042 🚌 Access by bus from Positano, or boat from Positano, Amalfi and Salerno

Music on the Rocks

This stylish nightclub, overlooking the east end of the beach, is the place to come for relaxed piano-bar music and traditional disco sounds.

✉ Grotta dell'Incanto 51, Amalfi ☎ 089 875 874 🕐 Closed Oct–Mar

Roccocò

Amalfi's best bet for a night on the dance floor if you can't be bothered to hop on the boat to Africana (see above).

✉ Via delle Carteire 98, Amalfi ☎ 089 873 080 🕐 Closed Sun–Thu Nov–Mar

SPORT

DIVING

Centro Sub Costiera Amalfitana

A highly professional dive school that offers courses for all levels and organizes both day and night dives in the marine park. Diving along this coast is recognized as being extremely beautiful due to the clarity of the water and light; depths up to 40m (130ft).

✉ Via Marina di Praia, Praiano, Positano ☎ 089 812 148; www.centrosub.it

SAILING AND WATER SKIING

Amalfi Boats

Charter, sailing and small boat rentals for exploring the coast and Capri, either with a captain and crew or on your own. Also offers water-skiing and fishing trips, and the boats can pick up at any of the villages along the coast.

✉ Via Monte 3, Minori, Amalfi ☎ 329 214 9811; www.amalfiboattours.com

Sight Locator Index

This index relates to the maps on the covers. We have given map references to the main sights of interest in the book. Grid references in italics indicate sights featured on the regional maps. Some sights within towns may not be plotted on the maps.

Index

Acknowledgements

The Automobile Association would like to thank the following photographers, companies and picture libraries for their assistance in the preparation of this book.

Abbreviations for the picture credits are as follows – (t) top; (b) bottom; (c) centre; (l) left; (r) right; (AA) AA World Travel Library.

6/7 Spanish Quarter, AA/M Jourdan; **8/9** Fishing boat, AA/M Jourdan; **10t** Pompei, AA/M Jourdan; **10c** Moped, AA/M Jourdan; **10/11** Caserta Palace Gardens, AA/M Jourdan; **11tl** Street scene, AA/M Jourdan; **11tr** Castel dell' Ovo, AA/M Jourdan; **11cr** Nuns, AA/M Jourdan; **11b** Local men, AA/M Jourdan; **12t** Fish Market, AA/M Jourdan; **12b** Fruit and vegetable stall, AA/M Jourdan; **12/3t** Seafood, AA/M Jourdan; **13c** Food shop, AA/M Jourdan; **13b** Pizza, AA/C Sawyer; **14tl** Seafood, AA/T Souter; **14cl** Cooking pizza, AA/M Jourdan; **14br** Sardines, AA/T Souter; **14/5t** Lorry, AA/M Jourdan; **14/5b** Meat and cheese stall, AA/M Jourdan; **15** Coffee, AA/M Jourdan; **16/7t** Pizza, AA/C Sawyer; **16/7b** Café, AA/M Jourdan; **18tl** Villa Cimbrone, AA/M Jourdan; **18bl** Museo di Capodimonte, AA/M Jourdan; **18tr** Via San Gregorio Armeno, AA/M Jourdan; **19t** Amalfi Coast, AA/M Jourdan; **19c** Pompei, AA/C Sawyer; **19b** Sorrento, AA/M Jourdan; **20/1** Moped, AA/M Jourdan; **24** Easter Parade, AA/M Jourdan; **25** Pizza, AA/M Jourdan; **28** Policeman, AA/M Jourdan; **30** Telephone box, AA/M Jourdan; **32** Policewoman, AA/M Jourdan; **34/5** Gardens at the Museo di Capodimonte, AA/M Jourdan; **36** Detail of a door at the Duomo di Amalfi, AA/M Jourdan; **36/7** Duomo di Amalfi, AA/M Jourdan; **38/9** Grotto Azzurra, World Pictures; **40/1** Monte Vesuvio, AA/T Souter; **41** Eruption of Vesuvius, AA; **42/3** Museo Archeologico di Napoli, Robert Harding Picture Library; **44** Museo di Capodimonte; AA/M Jourdan; **44/5** Museo di Capodimonte; AA/M Jourdan; **46** Positano, AA/M Jourdan; **46/7t** Ceramic plates, AA/M Jourdan; **46/7b** Positano, AA/C Sawyer; **48/9** Naples, AA/M Jourdan; **50/1** Tempio di Nettuno, AA/T Souter; **52/3** Villa dei Misteri in Pompei, Robert Harding Picture Library; **54/5** Villa Rufolo, AA/M Jourdan; **56/7** Pompei, AA/M Jourdan; **58/9** Via Chiaia, AA/M Jourdan; **59** Food and drink stall, AA/M Jourdan; **60/1** Restaurant, AA/M Jourdan; **62** Kayaking, AA/D Miterdiri; **65** Via Tribunali, AA/M Jourdan; **66/7** Positano, AA/M Jourdan; **68** Via San Gregorio Armeno, AA/M Jourdan; **70/1** Santa Chiara, AA/M Jourdan; **72** Pompei, AA/M Jourdan; **75** Palazzo Reale, AA/M Jourdan; **76** Ice cream, AA/S McBride; **78/9** Palazzo Reale, AA/M Jourdan; **80/1** Naples, AA/M Jourdan; **83** Via San Gregorio Armeno, AA/M Jourdan; **84/5** Castel Nuovo, AA/M Jourdan; **86/7** Castel Nuovo, AA/M Jourdan; **88** Certosa di San Martino, AA/M Jourdan: **90/1** Via San Gregorio Armeno, AA/M Jourdan; **91** Via San Gregorio Armeno, AA/M Jourdan; **92/3** Duomo, AA/M Jourdan; **94/5** Galleria Umberto I, AA/M Jourdan; **96/7** Palazzo Reale, AA/M Jourdan; **98/9** San Domenico Maggiore, AA/M Jourdan; **99** San Domenico Maggiore, AA/M Jourdan; **100** Santa Chiara, AA/M Jourdan; **100/1** Santa Chiara, AA/M Jourdan; **102** Castel dell'Ovo, AA/M Jourdan; **102/3** Santa Lucia, AA/M Jourdan; **104/5** Teatro San Carlo, CuboImages srl/Alamy; **106** Villa Floridiana, AA/M Jourdan; **115** Bay of Naples, AA/M Jourdan; **116** Capri, World Pictures; **118** Capri, World Pictures; **120** Herculaneum, AA/M Jourdan; **122/3** Ischia, World Pictures; **125** Sorrento, AA/C Sawyer; **126/7** Pompei, AA/M Jourdan; **128t** Pompei, AA/M Jourdan; **128b** Pompei, AA/M Jourdan **128/9** Pompei, AA/M Jourdan; **131** Sorrento, AA/C Sawyer; **132** Countryside near Massa Lubrense, AA/M Jourdan; **133** Building near Massa Lubrense, AA/M Jourdan; **137** Ravello, AA/M Jourdan; **138/9** Amalfi, AA/T Souter; **139t** Amalfi, AA/M Jourdan; **139b** Duomo di Amalfi, AA/C Sawyer; **140/1** Paestum, AA/T Souter; **142** Positano, AA/M Jourdan; **144** Ravello, AA/M Jourdan, **146** Salerno, AA/M Trelawny.

Every effort has been made to trace the copyright holders, and we apologise in advance for any accidental errors. We would be happy to apply the corrections in the following edition of this publication.

Street Index

Dear Reader

Your comments, opinions and recommendations are very important to us. Please help us to improve our travel guides by taking a few minutes to complete this simple questionnaire.

You do not need a stamp (unless posted outside the UK). If you do not want to cut this page from your guide, then photocopy it or write your answers on a plain sheet of paper.

Send to: **The Editor, AA World Travel Guides, FREEPOST SCE 4598, Basingstoke RG21 4GY.**

Your recommendations...

We always encourage readers' recommendations for restaurants, nightlife or shopping – if your recommendation is used in the next edition of the guide, we will send you a **FREE AA Guide** of your choice from this series. Please state below the establishment name, location and your reasons for recommending it.

____

____

____

____

____

____

Please send me **AA Guide** _______________

About this guide...

Which title did you buy?

AA _______________

Where did you buy it? _______________

When? m m / y y

Why did you choose this guide? _______________

____

____

____

____

Did this guide meet your expectations?

Exceeded ☐ Met all ☐ Met most ☐ Fell below ☐

Were there any aspects of this guide that you particularly liked? _______________

____

____

____

continued on next page...

Is there anything we could have done better? ______________________

____

____

____

About you...

Name (*Mr/Mrs/Ms*) ______________________

Address ______________________

____

______________________ Postcode ______________________

Daytime tel nos ______________________

Email ______________________

Please only give us your mobile phone number or email if you wish to hear from us about other products and services from the AA and partners by text or mms, or email.

Which age group are you in?

Under 25 ☐ 25–34 ☐ 35–44 ☐ 45–54 ☐ 55–64 ☐ 65+ ☐

How many trips do you make a year?

Less than one ☐ One ☐ Two ☐ Three or more ☐

Are you an AA member? Yes ☐ No ☐

About your trip...

When did you book? m m / y y When did you travel? m m / y y

How long did you stay? ______________________

Was it for business or leisure? ______________________

Did you buy any other travel guides for your trip? ______________________

If yes, which ones? ______________________

____

____

Thank you for taking the time to complete this questionnaire. Please send it to us as soon as possible, and remember, you do not need a stamp (*unless posted outside the UK*).

The information we hold about you will be used to provide the products and services requested and for identification, account administration, analysis, and fraud/loss prevention purposes. More details about how that information is used is in our privacy statement, which you'll find under the heading "Personal Information" in our terms and conditions and on our website: www.theAA.com. Copies are also available from us by post, by contacting the Data Protection Manager at AA, Fanum House, Basing View, Basingstoke, Hampshire RG21 4EA.

We may want to contact you about other products and services provided by us, or our partners (by mail, telephone or email) but please tick the box if you DO NOT wish to hear about such products and services from us by mail, telephone or email. ☐